The Book On

# Woke

## The Currency of Outrage and the Cost of Virtue

The Book On Series

## Jordan Ellis

Published by The Book On Publishing, 2025.

First edition. October 28, 2025

Website: https://thebookon.ca

Substack: https://thebookonpublishing.substack.com/

The Book On Woke: The Currency of Outrage and the Cost of Virtue
First edition. October 28, 2025

ISBN: 978-1-997909-45-3

Written by Jordan Ellis

# Other Books in The Book On Series

The Book On Life Unscripted
The Book On Risk Management in Payments
The Book On AI for Everyday People
The Book On Relationships
The Book On Master The Algorithm
The Book On Saying No
The Book On Community-Led Strategy
The Book On The Myth of Multitasking
The Book On The Burnout Blueprint
The Book On The Digital Reboot
The Book On The Shape of What's Coming
The Book On Strategic Obsession
The Book On High-Stakes Thinking
The Book On Artificial Leverage
The Book On Clarity
The Book On Uncertainty
The Book On Operational Excellence
The Book On Escape
The Book On Reinvention After Consequences
The Book On Re-Unifying Society
The Book On Taking Flight
The Book On Persuasion
The Book On Enough
The Book On Attention
The Book On Men (for Women)
The Book On Women (for Men)
The Book On The Cookbook for Cannibals

# Table of Contents

# Chapter 1: Awakening to Awareness: The Origin of Wokeness

The word "woke" didn't start in a hashtag. It didn't emerge from a think tank or a university seminar. It came from vernacular necessity, from Black communities in America who needed language to describe a specific kind of consciousness. To be woke, in its earliest iterations, meant you saw through the official story. You understood that the machinery of society didn't operate on the fairness it advertised. You recognized patterns invisible to those who'd never had reason to doubt the system. This wasn't performative awareness. This was survival intelligence, the kind developed when your safety depends on reading social environments that most people navigate unthinkingly. The term carried weight because it described something real: the moment when you stop accepting surface narratives and start questioning the architecture beneath them. It was a wake-up call from a dream that only felt like reality to those who'd never been shaken from it.

The etymology matters because it reveals what we've lost. "Woke" derives from African American Vernacular English, specifically the phrase "stay woke," which circulated in Black communities throughout the twentieth century. Lead Belly used it in a 1938 song warning about the Scottsboro Boys' wrongful convictions. Novelist William Melvin Kelley explored it in a 1962 New York Times article about white appropriation of Black culture, a bitter irony given what would later happen to the term itself. By the 1960s and 70s, "stay woke" meant maintaining vigilance against systemic injustice, particularly police violence and institutional racism. It wasn't a badge you wore. It was a posture you maintained. The grammar itself, "stay woke," not "become woke", implied constant effort, active attention, the recognition that awareness isn't a destination but a practice. You didn't achieve wokeness and rest. You stayed awake because the conditions requiring that consciousness persisted.

What made the original formulation powerful was its specificity. To be woke meant understanding particular mechanisms of oppression, redlining, mass incarceration, educational inequality, and employment discrimination. It meant seeing how systems that claimed neutrality consistently produced racialized outcomes. This wasn't abstract theory. This was pattern recognition born from lived experience and historical memory. When someone said "stay woke" about police interactions, they meant: understand that the encounter operates under different rules for you, that compliance doesn't guarantee safety, and that the official narrative about what happened will probably erase crucial context. When applied to employment, it meant: recognize that "culture fit" often codes for racial exclusion, that credentials don't shield you from bias, that your success threatens some people's sense of order. The term functioned as shorthand for accumulated wisdom about navigating systems designed without you in mind, or designed explicitly to constrain you.

## From Margin to Mainstream

The transformation began in earnest after Trayvon Martin's murder in 2012 and the subsequent acquittal of George Zimmerman in 2013. When activists created #BlackLivesMatter, "stay woke" became part of the movement's vocabulary, a reminder to maintain awareness of systemic violence against Black communities. Social media amplified the term beyond its original context. Suddenly, "woke" was traveling through networks that had never encountered it, picked up by people who lacked the historical and cultural framework that gave it meaning. This should have been a straightforward cultural exchange, marginalized communities sharing hard-won insights with broader audiences. But something strange happened in translation. The term began detaching from its specific referents and becoming a floating signifier for general progressive awareness. You could be "woke" about climate change, woke about mental health, woke about literally any social issue. The specificity dissolved. The grammar shifted from "stay woke" to "I'm woke," from continuous practice to achieved identity.

This linguistic drift wasn't accidental. It reflected a deeper phenomenon: the absorption of radical critique into mainstream culture through a process that simultaneously celebrates and neutralizes it. Being "woke" started attracting social capital, particularly in progressive spaces and among younger demographics. Corporations noticed. Media companies noticed. Politicians noticed. By 2016, the term had escaped containment entirely. Brands used it in advertising. Television shows referenced it. Think pieces proliferated. And with each iteration, the term became more abstracted from its origins, more amenable to performance, less tethered to the kind of sustained attention and structural analysis it originally demanded. What began as a warning about specific forms of systemic violence became a general marker of being "on the right side" of social issues. This transformation should trouble anyone who cares about the original insight.

The mainstreaming accelerated after 2016, turbocharged by the political climate and social media's reward structures. To declare yourself woke became a form of identity signaling, a shortcut to moral status that required less actual engagement with systemic analysis than it did public demonstration of having the right opinions. The platforms are optimized for this. Twitter's architecture rewarded hot takes about injustice more than sustained organizing. Instagram made activism photogenic, turning protests into aesthetic content. TikTok compressed complex social analysis into sixty-second explainers that flattened nuance in pursuit of viral reach. The incentive structures shifted. The original formulation of wokeness required you to see things that made you uncomfortable, including your own complicity in systems of oppression. The new version lets you announce your awareness without necessarily changing anything about how you operate in the world. You could be woke on your feed while maintaining perfectly conventional relationships to power in your actual life.

## The Machinery of Performance

What emerged was a predictable pattern, one that repeats whenever radical critique gets absorbed into mainstream culture. The language is preserved while the substance drains away. The form persists while the function inverts. You saw this with "revolution" in the 1960s: genuine calls for structural transformation became advertising copy for soft drinks and blue jeans. You saw it with "punk" in the 1970s, anti-establishment rage became a marketable aesthetic, sold back to alienated teenagers by the very corporations punk supposedly opposed. You saw it with "alternative" in the 1990s, underground culture became a demographic category, its rebellious content bleached away until "alternative" just meant "marketed to people who think of themselves as different." The pattern is so consistent it's almost boring. Oppositional consciousness gets discovered, commodified, stripped of threat, and sold as identity branding. What's remarkable about wokeness isn't that this happened; it's how quickly it happened, compressed by social media's metabolic rate into a transformation that took years instead of decades.

The performance machinery operates through several mechanisms, all of which corrode the original insight. First: the substitution of declaration for demonstration. In the original formulation, being woke meant you saw something, specific patterns, particular dynamics, concrete mechanisms of oppression. In the performance version, being woke means you say you see something. The focus shifts from the actual work of sustained attention to the public announcement that you're paying attention. This isn't a trivial distinction. Real awareness produces discomfort because it implicates you in systems you'd rather believe you stand outside of. It demands that you examine your own position within hierarchies of power. Performative wokeness offers the status benefits of moral awareness without the uncomfortable reckoning. You get to position yourself as enlightened while avoiding the destabilizing recognition that you, too, participate in and benefit from unjust arrangements.

Second: the multiplication of fronts without prioritization of depth. Once wokeness became detached from its specific origins, it could expand infinitely. You could, and were increasingly expected to, be woke about everything simultaneously. This sounds like progress. In practice, it meant trading depth for breadth, expertise for general awareness, focused action for diffuse concern. The original formulation accepted that you might be acutely conscious of some systems while still learning about others. The performance version demanded comprehensive wokeness; you needed the correct position on every social issue, preferably updated in real-time as the discourse evolved. This created exhausting moral surveillance, both internal and external. It also meant that being woke became more about tracking the shifting consensus in your social circles than about developing independent analysis. You weren't cultivating awareness through sustained engagement with particular injustices. You were keeping up with the discourse, making sure your positions aligned with whatever the current moment deemed acceptable.

Third: the transformation of awareness into a commodity. This is where it gets genuinely cynical. Once being woke carried social capital, markets developed to service that identity. Publishers rushed out books about social justice (many by authors who'd never done organizing work). Consultants offered corporate trainings in wokeness (usually repackaged HR compliance modules with new vocabulary). Influencers built platforms on performing wokeness (monetizing their political consciousness through brand partnerships and speaking fees). Clothing companies printed slogans on t-shirts. Streaming services greenlit shows about awakening. Universities added courses. The machinery of capitalism, remarkably efficient at absorbing critique and selling it back as lifestyle branding, captured wokeness and made it purchasable. You could buy your way into the identity. You could consume wokeness as content. This didn't just dilute the original insight; it inverted it entirely. What began as recognition of how systems operate to concentrate power became another product for those with resources to purchase.

## What We Lost in Translation

The distance between "stay woke" and "I'm woke" measures everything that went wrong. The original phrase assumed awareness was fragile, that you could slip back into comfortable narratives, that maintaining consciousness required effort and community. It built in humility; you had to stay woke because the alternative was falling back asleep. After all, the systems you were watching were designed to lull you into complacency. The reformulation as identity inverted this entirely. "I'm woke" suggests arrival, completion, a state achieved rather than a practice maintained. It centers the self, not "the system operates this way" but "I am the kind of person who sees." The grammar itself reveals the transformation from structural critique to personal identity, from collective vigilance to individual achievement. This isn't semantic nitpicking. The way we structure language shapes what becomes thinkable, what actions seem natural, and what problems come into focus.

What died in this translation was precisely what made the original insight valuable: its rootedness in specific historical conditions, its connection to actual communities navigating actual oppression, its insistence that awareness must connect to action rather than substitute for it. The original wokeness didn't let you off the hook by declaring your enlightenment. It demanded you do something with what you saw. It expected you to join organizations, show up to meetings, participate in campaigns, and take risks that actually cost you something. Being woke wasn't about accumulating the right opinions to display in the right spaces. It was about developing analytical capacity that informed strategic action. The performance version offers moral satisfaction without material consequence; you get to feel righteous without necessarily disrupting your relationship to power, comfort, or resources.

The story of how wokeness transformed from survival intelligence to social performance isn't just about one term's corruption. It's a case study in how systems absorb critique, how radical insights get defanged through mainstreaming, how language that names power relations gets repurposed to obscure them. It reveals the machinery that converts opposition into product, that takes tools developed by marginalized communities for their own liberation and repackages them as identity markers for the comfortable. Understanding this process isn't about mourning what was lost, though there's genuine loss here. It's about learning to recognize the pattern so we can interrupt it, so we can develop forms of consciousness and critique that resist easy absorption. Because the need that generated "stay woke" in the first place hasn't disappeared. The systems that require vigilance persist. But our ability to maintain that vigilance gets compromised when the language we use to name it becomes the very performance it was meant to penetrate.

The following chapters will dissect how this happened, the specific mechanisms through which awareness became currency, identity became brand, and justice became content. We'll examine how social media platforms architected performance, how institutions weaponized wokeness for their own purposes, and how language itself became a field of status competition. We'll look at what gets lost when empathy turns into game mechanics and virtue becomes a market position. But first, we needed to understand the origin point: what woke actually meant before it meant everything and nothing. That specificity matters. It's the measuring stick against which we can assess how far we've drifted, and what it might take to find our way back to something resembling the original insight, not out of nostalgia, but because the conditions that made "stay woke" necessary haven't changed. Only our ability to see them clearly has been compromised by the very language we created to name them.

## The Conservative Weaponization

But we're not done with the corruption yet. The progressive dilution of wokeness, its transformation into performative identity, created a vacuum that conservative forces rushed to fill. And here's where the story gets genuinely fascinating, in the way that watching a controlled demolition can be intriguing. Conservative media and politicians didn't just reject wokeness. They transformed it into a universal villain, an explanatory framework that could account for everything they opposed. "Woke" became the all-purpose enemy, the source of every cultural anxiety, the reason everything felt wrong to people who sensed they were losing cultural dominance. This wasn't a defensive reaction. This was a strategic deployment.

Watch how it works. Disney releases a film with a Black protagonist? That's woke. A brewery sponsors a trans influencer? Woke. Military recruitment focuses on diversity? Woke agenda. Do universities teach accurate history about slavery? Woke indoctrination. Climate scientists issue warnings? Woke hysteria. The term became infinitely elastic, capable of encompassing any cultural change that threatened traditional hierarchies or challenged comfortable narratives. What's clever about this rhetorical move is that it requires no actual engagement with the specific claims being made. You don't have to argue about whether systemic racism exists, whether trans people deserve protection, or whether climate change threatens civilization. You just label it "woke" and you've discredited it in the eyes of your audience. It's efficient. It's effective. It's completely detached from the term's origins, but that doesn't matter because the point isn't accuracy; it's weaponization.

This conservative deployment accelerated the term's meaninglessness while paradoxically giving it new power. Republicans running for office in 2022 and 2023 made "anti-woke" central to their campaigns, often without defining what they meant. Ron DeSantis built his presidential primary campaign around "Florida is where woke goes to die," positioning himself as the warrior against an enemy whose boundaries remained conveniently vague. This vagueness isn't a bug; it's a feature. When woke can mean anything that makes traditional conservatives uncomfortable, it becomes the perfect enemy. It's everywhere and nowhere. It explains cultural change without requiring you to understand the actual dynamics producing that change. It gives people a target for their anxiety without demanding they examine what's actually making them anxious.

The result is a perfect storm of meaninglessness. The progressive mainstream turned wokeness into performance, awareness as identity, justice as aesthetic, critique as brand. Conservative opposition turned it into a specter, a shapeshifting enemy that explains every unwelcome cultural shift. Both moves drain the term of its original analytical precision. Both substitute emotional reaction for structural understanding. And both, fascinatingly, serve existing power arrangements. The progressive performance version lets institutions claim enlightenment while changing very little about how resources and influence actually distribute. The conservative deployment version lets people resist changing anything while claiming they're defending principles rather than privilege.

## The Exhaustion Economy

There's a human cost to all this that doesn't get examined enough. The original "stay woke" acknowledged something real: that maintaining awareness is exhausting. Seeing systems clearly, especially systems you participate in, creates a psychological burden. That communities under threat need to sustain vigilance, which requires energy and mutual support. The communities that originated the term understood this. They built practices around it, organizing structures, cultural spaces, and mutual aid networks that helped people sustain consciousness without burning out.

The performance version and its conservative inverse both ignore this reality. They treat wokeness as either an achievement to display or an infection to purge, never as a practice that demands care and sustainability. Progressive spaces increasingly expect everyone to be maximally aware of every justice issue simultaneously, with no acknowledgment that this kind of comprehensive consciousness might be humanly impossible. You're supposed to be constantly educated, perpetually updated, and immediately responsive to the latest discourse shift. Fall behind and you risk callout, cancellation, and social death in your community. The incentive structure produces constant anxiety. Are your positions current? Did you miss the memo on which terminology is now problematic? Are you sufficiently vocal about the crisis that's trending today?

This creates what we might call the exhaustion economy, a system where moral status depends on displays of awareness that require unsustainable energy expenditure. People perform consciousness; they don't actually have time to develop. They post about issues they haven't studied because not posting signals indifference. They join campaigns they don't understand because visibility matters more than comprehension. The result isn't sustained engagement with injustice. It's burnout, resentment, and eventual withdrawal. Or worse: it's cynicism, the recognition that the performance matters more than the substance, that you're playing a game of appearances rather than actually confronting systems of power.

Meanwhile, the conservative deployment produces its own exhaustion. People constantly scan culture for evidence of woke infiltration, maintaining perpetual outrage at every perceived threat, organizing their entire political consciousness around opposition to a term that means nothing specific. This, too, burns people out. It keeps them angry without giving them anything constructive to build. It channels legitimate anxieties about economic precarity, social change, and loss of community into culture war battles that don't actually address the material conditions producing those anxieties. Both sides of this exhausted economy benefit someone, usually media companies, political operations, and consultants who profit from sustained engagement and polarization, but they don't help the people caught in the machinery.

## Reclaiming Precision

So what do we do? We could abandon the term entirely, accept it's too corrupted to salvage. There's logic to this. Sometimes language becomes so compromised that continuing to use it just perpetuates confusion. But there's another option: we could insist on precision. We could refuse both the progressive vagueness and the conservative weaponization. We could return to asking what specific awareness we're talking about, what particular systems we're examining, what concrete actions emerge from that consciousness. This doesn't mean trying to resurrect the original "stay woke"; that moment has passed, and attempting nostalgic recovery usually fails. It means learning from what made that formulation powerful and applying those principles to how we talk about awareness now.

Precision means specificity. Not "I'm woke" but "I'm paying attention to how housing policy produces segregation." Not "that's woke" but "that challenges traditional gender hierarchies." Not "woke indoctrination" but "teaching that makes me uncomfortable because it contradicts what I learned." Force the specificity. Name the actual phenomenon. Describe the concrete system. This doesn't resolve all political disagreements; people can understand the same system and reach different conclusions about what to do. But it eliminates the meaningless abstraction that lets wokeness become whatever anyone needs it to be in the moment. It restores the possibility of actual debate rather than symbolic warfare.

Precision also means accepting limits. Nobody can maintain acute awareness of every injustice simultaneously. The original "stay woke" accepted this; it asked you to remain conscious of specific threats in specific contexts. We need to rebuild that humility. It's fine to focus your attention. It's necessary, even. Better to develop a deep understanding of particular systems than a superficial awareness of everything. Better to take meaningful action on issues you've actually studied than to express concern about everything trending. This isn't permission to ignore injustice you're not personally focused on. It's recognition that sustainable engagement requires boundaries, that you can't maintain vigilance about everything, that attempting to do so produces the exhaustion economy that benefits no one except those profiting from your perpetual anxiety.

# Chapter 2: From Awareness to Performance: The Evolution of Social Justice

Social justice didn't begin as a performance. It started as organized resistance, people using institutional power to challenge institutional power. The evolution from that foundation to what we see today represents one of the most fascinating transformations in modern political culture: how movements built on material demands became movements built on symbolic gestures, how collective action fragmented into individual virtue displays, and how the pursuit of structural change gave way to the curation of personal righteousness.

Consider the timeline. The 1960s Civil Rights Movement operated through sit-ins, boycotts, voter registration drives, and legal challenges, tactics designed to impose economic and political costs until systems changed. The anti-apartheid divestment campaigns of the 1980s forced universities and corporations to withdraw capital from South Africa, applying financial pressure that contributed to regime collapse. ACT UP in the late 1980s disrupted pharmaceutical companies and government agencies until they accelerated AIDS drug development and treatment access. These movements shared a common architecture: identify the power structure maintaining injustice, develop tactics that force that structure to bear costs, and maintain pressure until material conditions change. Success meant legislative victories, institutional policy shifts, and resource redistribution. Failure meant nothing changed except how you felt about yourself.

Now examine the 2020s equivalent. A corporation changes its social media avatar to a rainbow flag for Pride Month. An individual adds pronouns to their email signature. Someone posts a black square on Instagram during a racial justice protest. A brand releases a commercial celebrating diversity. These actions dominate contemporary social justice performance, yet they share a defining characteristic: they impose no costs on existing power structures. They require no sacrifice from the performer. They create no material change in how resources, opportunities, or power are distributed across society. They operate entirely in the realm of symbol, where the appearance of alignment with justice substitutes for the substance of challenging injustice.

## The Architecture of Performative Justice

The transformation didn't happen overnight. It emerged from the convergence of three separate developments that each seemed innocuous, even positive, until they fused into something altogether different.

First: the professionalization of activism. By the 1990s, social justice work increasingly meant working for nonprofits dependent on foundation grants and donor relationships. This created organizational incentives to demonstrate measurable outcomes, workshops delivered, trainings conducted, awareness raised, rather than power challenged. A nonprofit that successfully blocked a harmful policy implementation might struggle to quantify that victory for grant applications. A nonprofit that conducted fifty diversity trainings for corporate clients could easily generate impressive metrics. The latter model proved far more fundable. As activism professionalized, it optimized for activities that satisfied donors and generated data, not necessarily for activities that redistributed power. The institutional DNA shifted from disruption toward service provision, from agitation toward education, from confrontation toward consultation.

Second: the digitization of social life. When political expression migrated onto social platforms designed to maximize engagement, it encountered an environment that rewarded certain behaviors and punished others. Nuanced arguments about policy details generate modest engagement. Moral outrage performs exceptionally well. Detailed analysis of systemic problems reaches limited audiences. Personal testimony about experiencing injustice goes viral. Long-term organizing work that builds power gradually remains invisible. Dramatic confrontations that produce shareable moments dominate feeds. The platforms didn't create performative politics, but they made an ecosystem where performative politics outcompeted everything else for attention, distribution, and social reward.

Over time, activists optimized their tactics for platform success, which meant optimizing for performance rather than power-building.

Third: the expansion of higher education and the institutionalization of critical theory. As concepts developed in academic contexts, intersectionality, microaggressions, privilege frameworks, and identity categories entered broader discourse, they underwent translation. Academic frameworks designed for analyzing power structures became personal identity markers. Theoretical concepts meant to illuminate systemic patterns became individual moral categories. Language developed to critique institutions became language for critiquing individuals. The migration of academic vocabulary into popular usage wasn't inherently problematic, but it occurred without the methodological rigor that made those concepts useful in their original context. "Intersectionality" describes how systems of oppression interconnect and produce distinct experiences at their crossroads. In popular usage, it became a hierarchy of identity categories determining whose voice carries authority in any discussion. The academic tool became a social ranking system.

These three streams merged. Professional activists needed a demonstrable impact for funding. Digital platforms rewarded visible moral performance. Academic frameworks provided sophisticated-sounding language that signaled education and awareness. The result: social justice evolved from a practice focused on changing institutions into a practice focused on demonstrating personal virtue within institutions. The target shifted from the architecture of power to the performance of alignment with those who claim to oppose that architecture.

## The Mechanics of Performance

Performative social justice operates according to distinct mechanics that differentiate it from justice work aimed at material change. Understanding these mechanics clarifies why contemporary social justice often feels simultaneously omnipresent and ineffectual, why it generates constant activity yet produces limited structural transformation.

The first mechanic is substitution: symbolic action replaces material action, then claims equivalent moral weight. A company that issues a statement supporting racial justice while maintaining hiring practices that exclude Black candidates from senior positions performs substitution. The statement costs nothing, risks nothing, changes nothing, but it purchases the appearance of commitment. The performance substitutes for the substance. Critically, this substitution doesn't typically involve conscious cynicism. Most performers genuinely believe the symbolic gesture carries moral weight. They've internalized an environment where symbolic alignment counts as meaningful action, where declaring the right position equals fighting for that position. The substitution becomes invisible to those performing it.

The second mechanism is individual atomization: collective action fragments into personal moral management. Instead of organizing to challenge an exploitative corporate practice, individuals check whether they're shopping at the right stores, buying the right products, and supporting the right businesses. The scale collapses from structural to individual, the method shifts from organized pressure to consumer choice, and the objective transforms from changing how institutions operate to maintaining personal ethical purity. This atomization serves power perfectly. An organized movement demanding wage increases threatens capital. Thousands of individuals carefully curating their consumer ethics according to overlapping and contradictory criteria pose no threat whatsoever. They're too busy monitoring their own virtue to build collective power.

The third mechanic is language inflation: vocabulary proliferates while precision collapses. The discourse generates endless new terms, microaggression, tone policing, centering, platforming, emotional labor, and gaslighting, often repurposing clinical or theoretical language for everyday interpersonal conflicts. This vocabulary inflation serves several functions simultaneously. It signals group membership, demonstrating that you know the codes. It transforms ordinary disagreements into moral emergencies, escalating stakes and obviating the need for good-faith engagement with opposing views. It creates constant opportunities to correct others' language, providing the feeling of political action without requiring engagement with material politics. As the vocabulary multiplies, actual communication becomes more difficult. Conversations devolve into definitional disputes about which terms apply to which situations, debates about whether someone used language correctly, and arguments about who has standing to invoke which concepts. The political becomes linguistic, and linguistic precision becomes impossible because the terms change faster than shared definitions can stabilize.

The fourth mechanic is competitive victimhood: suffering becomes social capital. In traditional political organizing, highlighting injustice served strategic purposes, demonstrating need, building solidarity, and justifying demands for redress. In performative social justice, suffering becomes something different: a credential that authorizes speech and immunizes against criticism. The person who has suffered most gets to speak with the greatest authority and faces the least accountability. This creates perverse incentives. Rather than working to reduce suffering, individuals have an incentive to emphasize, amplify, or even exaggerate their experiences of harm. Rather than building coalitions across differences, groups compete to establish their relative victimization. Rather than developing thick skin and resilience as tools for long-term political struggle, fragility becomes a virtue because it demonstrates how much harm you've endured. The competitive dynamic inverts the traditional goal of justice movements. Instead of working toward a world with less suffering, the system rewards producing more claims of suffering.

## The Social Economy of Performance

Understanding performative social justice requires recognizing it as an economy, a system of production, exchange, and accumulation where specific goods trade to particular values within defined markets. The good being traded is virtue. The currency is attention and social status. The market is the networks, professional, social, and digital, where educated progressives congregate and compete.

Virtue production follows identifiable patterns. An individual identifies an injustice, ideally before others have noticed it. They articulate that injustice using the appropriate vocabulary. They signal their own awareness and righteousness by denouncing the injustice, calling out those perpetuating it, and demanding accountability. If the performance succeeds, they accumulate social capital: followers, engagement, recognition as someone who "gets it," and opportunities to speak or write about the issue. This capital can sometimes convert into material benefits, speaking fees, consulting contracts, career advancement, but often its value remains purely social. You become someone known for being on the right side.

The competitive dynamics of this economy create predictable distortions. Just as financial markets reward finding undervalued assets before others do, the virtue economy rewards discovering injustices before they become widely recognized. This creates an incentive to push boundaries, to identify ever-more-subtle forms of harm, to find oppression in places others haven't thought to look. The term "microaggression" emerged from this dynamic. Once obvious forms of discrimination faced widespread condemnation, the market demanded new frontiers, microaggressions, small, often ambiguous behaviors that might indicate bias, and provided new territory. But once microaggressions became widely recognized, the market demanded more. Now we have "micro-invalidations," "micro-insults," "micro-assaults," each subdividing further. The taxonomy expands because the market rewards novelty.

Competition also drives what economists call "preference falsification", publicly expressing views you don't privately hold because doing so carries social benefits or because expressing your actual views carries social costs. In the virtue economy, preference falsification becomes widespread. People publicly embrace positions they privately question because they've watched what happens to those who express doubt. They express certainty about complex issues because admitting uncertainty appears as moral weakness. They adopt the latest vocabulary even when it seems counterproductive because using last year's language marks you as behind. This creates an environment where public discourse and private belief increasingly diverge, where almost everyone feels they can't say what they actually think, but everyone continues performing what they believe they're supposed to think.

The economy also produces specialization. Some individuals become virtue brokers, those who interpret whether specific actions or statements qualify as acceptable, who have the authority to grant or deny the label of "ally," and who can offer absolution or condemnation. These brokers accumulate power that derives entirely from their position within the social economy, not from any material capacity to change institutions. They can destroy reputations but can't improve material conditions. Their power depends on maintaining the economy's rules while simultaneously positioning themselves as authorities on those rules. They need injustice to persist so they can continue identifying it, interpreting it, and adjudicating responses to it.

## When Justice Becomes Brand Management

Perhaps nothing reveals the transformation more clearly than how institutions relate to social justice claims. Corporations, universities, media organizations, government agencies, and institutions that structure how power and resources are actually distributed have learned to deploy social justice language as a defense mechanism that insulates them from demands for structural change.

Consider the standard institutional response to social justice pressure. First comes the statement, carefully crafted, prominently displayed, expressing commitment to equity, inclusion, diversity, justice. The statement costs nothing and commits to nothing specific. Next comes the appointment of a Chief Diversity Officer, a task force, and a committee to examine the issue and develop recommendations. These positions rarely carry budget authority or policy-making power, but they create the appearance of institutional action. Then come the training workshops on bias, sessions on microaggressions, and education about identity and privilege. The training makes employees feel the institution takes these issues seriously while avoiding any discussion of how the institution actually distributes power and resources. Finally comes the metrics, diversity statistics displayed on websites, inclusion initiatives highlighted in annual reports, and awards for equity work prominently publicized.

Notice what's absent from this sequence: material redistribution. The institution never has to change who it hires for powerful positions, how it compensates different workers, what communities it invests in or extracts from, which populations it serves or excludes, or what practices it maintains that produce unequal outcomes. It manages the appearance of commitment to justice without bearing any costs that might arise from actual commitment to justice. The social justice vocabulary becomes a shield against demands for structural change.

This institutional adoption reveals the completeness of performance's victory over substance. When the language developed to challenge power becomes the language power uses to defend itself, when corporations can market social justice while maintaining practices that produce injustice, when institutions can brand themselves as progressive while operating according to regressive logics, the performance has achieved total victory. It no longer even competes with substantive justice work; it has fully replaced it in most institutional contexts.

The tragedy isn't that institutions cynically deploy social justice language while maintaining unjust practices. Many people within these institutions genuinely believe they're advancing justice through statements, trainings, and diversity metrics. The tragedy is that the performance has become so successful at simulating justice that most people can no longer distinguish between the simulation and the substance. They've forgotten that justice meant changing who has power and resources, not changing who uses which vocabulary while power and resources remain concentrated in the same hands.

The evolution from awareness to performance represents a triumph of institutional capture. Systems threatened by social justice movements learned to absorb the language of those movements, deploy that language as evidence of alignment with justice, and thereby neutralize demands for actual change. The performance isn't a betrayal of social justice; it's the predictable outcome of how power adapts to challenges. And the adaptation worked spectacularly. We now live in a world where social justice language saturates institutional communications. At the same time, material inequality continues to intensify, where everyone is committed to equity while resources flow upward, and where the vocabulary of transformation becomes the mechanism preserving what needs transforming.

## The Psychological Capture

The institutional capture has a psychological counterpart that may prove more consequential. When performance becomes indistinguishable from practice, something happens to the performer's internal calibration. The person who spends years performing social justice, posting the right statements, using the correct language, attending the approved workshops, and denouncing the designated villains begins to experience their performance as substantive action. The gap between what they're doing and what actually changes becomes invisible to them.

This isn't hypocrisy in the traditional sense. Hypocrisy requires knowing the difference between your stated values and your actual behavior. What we're witnessing operates at a deeper level, a genuine dissolution of the category distinction between symbolic and material action. The corporate executive who approves a Black Lives Matter statement while maintaining hiring practices that exclude Black candidates from leadership isn't consciously lying. They've internalized an environment where issuing the statement constitutes meaningful anti-racist action. The university administrator who creates a diversity initiative while preserving admissions and funding structures that entrench class advantages isn't deliberately perpetuating inequality. They believe they're fighting inequality through the initiative. The psychological capture is complete when you can't perceive the contradiction because the performance has fully replaced the substance in your mental model of what justice work means.

This dissolution creates a peculiar consequence: the more someone performs social justice, the more immune they become to recognizing their complicity in injustice. Each performance reinforces their self-concept as someone who fights for justice. That reinforced self-concept makes them less capable of recognizing how their actual institutional position and behaviors might perpetuate the systems they believe they oppose. The performance doesn't just fail to produce change, it actively inhibits the psychological capacity to recognize that failure. You can't see what you're not doing when you're convinced that what you are doing counts as doing it.

Consider how this operates in professional contexts. Publishing has spent the past decade engaged in intensive social justice performance, diversity statements, bias training, mentorship programs, panels about representation, and awards recognizing inclusive excellence. Meanwhile, the industry has contracted around an increasingly narrow class position. Stable publishing jobs are concentrated in expensive coastal cities. Entry-level positions either pay poverty wages or operate as unpaid internships. Career advancement depends on networking access, cultural capital, and the ability to absorb years of financial precarity, filters that systematically exclude working-class candidates regardless of race or identity. The performance intensifies as the material conditions become more exclusionary. And the people performing most enthusiastically are often those most insulated by class privilege, least able to recognize how their industry's basic economics produce the exclusions their diversity initiatives claim to address.

The psychological mechanism operates like this: intensive performance creates psychological investment in the performance's adequacy. Admitting the performance doesn't constitute real action would require admitting you've wasted years on meaningless gestures while actual injustice persisted. That admission carries an enormous psychological cost. It's easier, more psychologically sustainable, to defend the performance's significance, to insist that awareness matters, that representation matters, that having difficult conversations matters. All these things do matter, in limited ways, but they matter infinitely less than material redistribution of power and resources. The performer can't afford to acknowledge that difference because doing so would collapse their self-concept. So they defend the performance with increasing fervor, and that defense calcifies into genuine belief. The performance becomes unfalsifiable.

# Chapter 3: Identity Politics: From Representation to Status Signaling

Identity politics began with a simple premise: groups excluded from power needed a collective organization to claim their share of it. Women, racial minorities, LGBTQ individuals, and disabled people weren't abstract categories but concrete constituencies denied access to resources, opportunities, and decision-making authority. The logic was straightforward: if individual merit couldn't overcome structural barriers, then group solidarity might. If the system ignored isolated voices, then coordinated demands might force a response. This wasn't about feelings or recognition or visibility. It was about seats at the table, dollars in budgets, laws on books, and bodies in positions of authority. Identity politics meant organizing around shared characteristics to achieve material redistribution of power. It meant leveraging collective identity as a tool for forcing institutions to change how they allocated resources and opportunities. The measure of success was concrete: Did more women get hired into executive positions? Did more Black families secure mortgages? Did LGBTQ individuals gain legal protections? The identity part was the organizing principle; the politics part was the objective.

Somewhere between that foundation and today, something fundamental shifted. Identity politics didn't disappear; it metastasized into something that looks similar from a distance but operates according to entirely different mechanics. What started as a strategy for achieving material gains became an end in itself. The focus migrated from changing institutional structures to establishing social hierarchies within activist spaces. The question shifted from "what power are we building?" to "who gets to speak?" The victories that mattered stopped being legislative or institutional and became symbolic: who appears in which advertisement, who gets quoted in which article, whose terminology becomes standard, whose interpretation of events becomes authoritative. Identity transformed from an organizing tool into a status marker, and politics transformed from a power struggle into a status competition. The result is a system that generates endless motion while changing remarkably little about how resources, opportunities, and authority actually distribute across society.

## The Status Hierarchy of Oppression

Contemporary identity politics operates on a currency system where marginalized identities function as social capital. But not all identities carry equal value in this economy, and the exchange rates shift according to rules that have nothing to do with actual political power or material deprivation. Instead, they follow the logic of what sociologists call "stigma competition", a process where groups compete to establish their relative position in hierarchies of victimization. The group that can claim the most oppression, the most urgent suffering, the most historical injustice gains moral authority, conversational priority, and immunity from criticism. This creates a perverse marketplace where suffering becomes valuable and groups have an incentive to emphasize rather than minimize their victimization.

Watch how this plays out in practice. A meeting convenes to address workplace inequality. Before substantive discussion begins, participants establish their credentials, not their expertise or experience with the specific issue, but their identity markers. Someone identifies as a queer woman of color. Another identifies as neurodivergent and disabled. A third mentions being a first-generation immigrant. These aren't incidental biographical details; they're bids in a status auction. Each declaration stakes a claim to authority based on accumulated marginalization. The person with the most oppression checkmarks gets to speak first, at greatest length, with least pushback. Their perspective carries automatic weight regardless of whether they've studied the issue, worked in the relevant field, or demonstrated any particular insight. The identity credentials substitute for substantive credentials, and the conversation optimizes for recognizing suffering rather than solving problems.

This hierarchy creates predictable distortions. First, it incentivizes identity proliferation. As certain identities become widely recognized and their oppression claims become established, the status value of those identities declines. The market demands novelty. This explains the explosive growth in identity categories and subcategories, not because human experience suddenly became more diverse, but because the status economy rewards discovering or articulating previously unnamed identities. Each new category, each new subdivision, represents fresh territory where early adopters can claim pioneering status. The person who identifies as demisexual gains a status advantage over someone who simply identifies as queer, because the former demonstrates more sophisticated awareness of identity nuance. The proliferation serves status competition, not descriptive accuracy.

Second, the hierarchy incentivizes grievance escalation. If status derives from oppression, and oppression manifests through harm, then identifying harm becomes a profitable social activity. This doesn't mean the harm isn't real; much of it certainly is. But it means the system rewards finding harm, naming harm, amplifying harm, and competing over whose harm registers as most severe. A colleague uses the wrong pronoun: microaggression. A professor assigns a reading from dead white men: Epistemic Violence. A policy decision doesn't explicitly center marginalized voices: structural oppression. The terminology escalates to match the status stakes. What might once have been described as mistakes, oversights, or differences in perspective become violence, trauma, and harm. The language inflation serves a purpose: it establishes severity, which establishes status, which establishes authority.

Third, the hierarchy incentivizes intersectional accounting, the practice of tallying oppression markers like a poker hand. Someone who checks one marginalization box has less status than someone who checks three. This creates what scholars call "oppression Olympics," where individuals compete to accumulate the most disadvantaged identity combination. The practice reaches its logical conclusion in social media bios that read like résumés of marginalization: "disabled nonbinary Latine neurodivergent survivor." Each term adds status points. Each term deflects potential criticism. Each term establishes standing to speak on issues increasingly distant from the actual identities listed. The multiplication of identity markers becomes a shield and a sword, protection against challenge and authorization to challenge others.

## The Performance of Authenticity

What makes contemporary identity politics particularly sophisticated is how it manages the problem of authenticity. Early identity politics faced a simpler landscape: membership in a group was relatively clear-cut. You were Black or you weren't. You were a woman or you weren't. You were gay or you weren't. These categories, while socially constructed and historically contingent, had relatively stable boundaries in their immediate contexts. But as identity politics evolved into status competition, the value of identity markers increased, which created an incentive for boundary expansion and claims to membership. Simultaneously, the proliferation of identity categories meant that many identities became unverifiable through external observation. This combination, increased value plus decreased verifiability, created the perfect conditions for what we might call identity arbitrage: claiming identities that carry status benefits without the material costs that originally generated those identities' moral claims.

Consider the phenomenon of "ethnic ambiguity" in professional contexts. A person with one grandparent from a marginalized group leverages that ancestry to check diversity boxes on applications, claim minority status in scholarships, and access opportunities designated for underrepresented groups, despite growing up with full socioeconomic privilege and no direct experience of the discrimination that justified those programs. Universities encounter students who discover Indigenous ancestry just in time for college applications. Corporations encounter executives who suddenly emphasize ethnic backgrounds that went unmentioned during their entire careers until diversity initiatives made such backgrounds advantageous. The opportunism isn't always conscious or cynical. Often, it involves a genuine exploration of heritage. But the timing reveals the incentive structure: identity becomes valuable, so people suddenly discover they have claims to valuable identities.

The problem intensifies with identities that are entirely self-reported and require no external validation. Consider the explosion in people identifying as nonbinary. Some percentage surely experience genuine dysphoria or discomfort with binary gender categories. But the rate of increase, particularly among young people in progressive spaces, suggests something beyond individual gender experience. It suggests social contagion and status seeking. Declaring oneself nonbinary costs nothing in progressive environments while conferring immediate benefits: membership in a marginalized group, authority to speak on gender issues, immunity from being dismissed as just another privileged person. The declaration requires no medical diagnosis, no social transition, no material sacrifice. Change your pronouns on Slack, add "they/them" to your email signature, and you've secured status benefits that would take actual marginalized groups generations to achieve through organized political action.

The system handles authenticity challenges through a clever mechanism: accusations of gatekeeping. Anyone who questions whether someone's claimed identity is genuine, or whether they've experienced the marginalization that supposedly generates moral authority, gets accused of policing boundaries. "You don't get to decide who's really [identity]" becomes the reflexive defense against scrutiny. This works because it deploys the language of inclusion and acceptance, core values in progressive spaces, to shut down questions about opportunism and fraud. The result is a system where identity claims are essentially unfalsifiable. To question them is to commit a moral violation worse than falsely claiming an identity for status benefits. The progressive commitment to respecting self-identification creates a loophole large enough to drive a truck through, and plenty of people have noticed.

## The Coalition Impossibility

Traditional identity politics, for all its limitations, contained internal logic about coalition-building. Different marginalized groups might form alliances based on shared interests in challenging power structures that disadvantaged them all. Labor unions brought together workers across ethnic and racial lines because they shared a material interest in higher wages and better conditions. The Civil Rights Movement attracted diverse supporters because the principle of equal treatment under the law applied broadly. These coalitions required compromise and negotiation; different groups had different priorities, and an alliance meant accepting that you wouldn't always get everything you wanted. But the shared objective of redistribution provided reason to maintain the coalition despite friction.

Contemporary identity politics makes coalition increasingly impossible because it operates on contradictory principles. Instead of shared material interest, it relies on recognition of relative oppression. Instead of compromising for collective gain, it demands that more privileged voices defer to more marginalized ones. Instead of building power through numbers, it subdivides into ever-smaller categories, each insisting on its unique perspective and specific needs. The more sophisticated the intersectional analysis becomes, the more it reveals conflicts between different marginalized groups and the less it provides tools for resolving those conflicts.

Watch what happens when different marginalized identities collide. Feminists organizing around sex-based rights conflict with trans activists organizing around gender identity. The feminist argument, that women as a class face specific oppression based on biological sex, directly contradicts the trans activist argument that gender identity, not biology, determines who counts as a woman. Both groups claim marginalization. Both claim their issue is urgent. Both claim the other group's position causes them harm. Traditional coalition politics might negotiate compromise: protect both sex-based rights in some contexts and gender identity in others, depending on specific stakes. Contemporary identity politics can't do this because compromise requires admitting that your group's needs aren't absolute, which undermines your claim to maximum oppression, which costs you status in the hierarchy.

Or consider conflicts between racial minorities and LGBTQ communities. Many immigrant communities from socially conservative countries hold traditional views on sexuality and gender. Progressive identity politics wants to support both immigrants against xenophobia and LGBTQ individuals against homophobia. But when immigrant communities express homophobic views, or when LGBTQ activists criticize immigrant communities' attitudes, the framework breaks. Who has a more oppressed status, the immigrant or the gay person? Whose perspective deserves deference? The oppression hierarchy can't resolve this because it's designed for comparing groups to dominant majorities, not for adjudicating conflicts between marginalized groups. When confronted with these contradictions, identity politics typically fragments rather than builds a coalition, with each group insisting the other isn't actually marginalized or is perpetuating oppression.

The coalition problem extends to class, the dimension identity politics systematically ignores. A working-class white man and an upper-middle-class Black woman might share economic interests: both benefit from higher minimum wages, stronger labor protections, more progressive taxation, and better public services. Traditional left politics would organize them together around those shared interests.

Contemporary identity politics can't make that coalition work because its framework says the white man has privilege and should defer to the Black woman. In contrast, the white man's actual lived experience involves economic precarity and lack of opportunity. He's told he has advantages he doesn't experience, while she leverages identity credentials to access opportunities unavailable to him. The framework generates resentment rather than solidarity, and material interests that might unite them get subordinated to status competitions that drive them apart.

## The Institutional Capture

The most revealing evidence that identity politics transformed from a redistribution mechanism to a status game appears in how institutions have absorbed it. If identity politics genuinely threatened existing power structures, those structures would resist it. Instead, they've embraced it enthusiastically, not because they've become more committed to justice, but because this version of identity politics poses no threat whatsoever to their fundamental operations. Corporations, universities, government agencies, media organizations, they've all integrated identity politics into their operations in ways that burnish their reputations while changing nothing about how they actually distribute resources and power.

Corporate diversity initiatives exemplify this perfectly. Companies spend millions on diversity training, hire Chief Diversity Officers, release annual diversity reports tracking demographic representation, sponsor employee resource groups, and issue statements supporting marginalized communities. These activities generate enormous performance, workshops, emails, events, metrics, and declarations. But examine what they don't change: wage structures, wealth distribution, executive composition, and power hierarchies. The diversity apparatus operates entirely at the level of representation and culture while leaving economic structures untouched. Amazon can sponsor Pride parades while fighting unionization. Facebook can hire a diverse workforce while generating profits from algorithms that spread hate. Goldman Sachs can require diverse slates for board positions while concentrating wealth in fewer hands. The commitment to identity politics involves no sacrifice of profit, no redistribution of ownership, no constraint on accumulation.

Universities demonstrate the same pattern. They've expanded bureaucracies dedicated to diversity, equity, and inclusion, administrators, offices, programs, and requirements. They've diversified student bodies and, to a lesser extent, faculty. They've revised curricula to include more perspectives from marginalized groups. They've implemented speech codes and bias reporting systems. All of this creates the appearance of institutions deeply committed to challenging oppression. Yet the fundamental economics haven't changed: tuition continues rising faster than inflation, saddling students with debt that disproportionately burdens those from poorer backgrounds. Adjunct faculty, disproportionately women and minorities, remain exploited with poverty wages and no security. Endowments grow through investments that profit from exactly the systems that generate the inequality the diversity apparatus purports to challenge. The university achieves moral satisfaction through diversity performance while maintaining economic models that reproduce class hierarchy.

The pattern repeats across institutions because it serves institutional interests perfectly. Identity politics, in its contemporary form, allows organizations to demonstrate progressive credentials without threatening their economic models or power structures. It's cheaper to hire a diversity officer than to raise wages. It's easier said than changed corporate governance. It's more comfortable to add marginalized voices to panels than to redistribute authority. The institution gets reputational benefits, protection against criticism, appeal to socially conscious consumers, and better rankings on diversity metrics while maintaining whatever practices actually generate its revenue and power. The people engaged in diversity work aren't necessarily cynical; many genuinely believe they're advancing justice. But the institutional logic ensures that their work channels toward symbolic change rather than material redistribution.

The capture reveals itself in who gets hired for these diversity positions. They're rarely organizers from grassroots movements or activists with track records of challenging institutional power. They're professionals who understand how to work within institutions, who speak the language of diversity but don't threaten disruption, who can translate political demands into administrative programs that look responsive while limiting actual change. They become intermediaries who absorb pressure from outside activists and pressure from below, translating both into bureaucratic processes that diffuse rather than concentrate power. The institution points to these positions as evidence of commitment while using them to prevent more fundamental challenges.

## The Exhaustion Point

Identity politics as status competition contains inherent contradictions that make it unsustainable. The more it succeeds in proliferating identity categories and raising awareness about marginalization, the more it accelerates its own collapse. Each new identity category subdivides the potential coalition further. Each new form of recognized oppression dilutes the moral weight of existing claims. Each new round of status competition ratchets up the performance requirements until they become impossible to meet. The system is eating itself, and the people most invested in it are starting to notice.

Consider the fatigue visible in progressive spaces. People are exhausted from constantly updating their language to avoid giving offense. People are anxious about navigating ever-more-complex rules about who can say what in which contexts. People are tired of watching conversations derail into identity credential-checking rather than addressing substance. People are frustrated that meetings accomplish nothing because they spend all their time processing feelings about group dynamics. This isn't backlash from conservatives or resistance from the powerful; this is exhaustion from people who signed up for social justice and found themselves trapped in endless status negotiations.

The fatigue reveals a deeper problem: identity politics as a status game provides no theory of victory. Traditional political organizing has endpoints, laws pass, policies change, institutions reform, and then you move to the next campaign. You can win, declare victory, and focus energy elsewhere. Status competition has no endpoint because status is relative and social hierarchies are ubiquitous. There's always another microaggression to identify, always another form of privilege to name, always another identity nuance to recognize, always another way someone's language or behavior could be more sensitive. The work is infinite because the objective is infinite: perfect awareness, perfect sensitivity, perfect recognition of all possible identities and their intersections. This isn't a campaign; it's a permanent state of vigilance that guarantees burnout.

The system also generates its own opposition, often from people it purports to represent. Working-class minorities who find identity politics irrelevant to their material needs. Immigrants who came from countries with actual oppression find American progressive terminology absurd. People from marginalized groups who succeeded through effort reject the narrative that their identity makes success impossible. These dissidents get labeled race traitors, internalized oppressors, people suffering from false consciousness, anything except what they often are, which is people whose lived experience doesn't match the theory. Their existence reveals that identity politics explains less about actual human experience than it claims, and their rejection of it undermines its authority.

What comes after identity politics isn't clear yet. Perhaps a return to material politics that subordinates identity to class interests. Maybe a reframing that uses identity as an organizing tool rather than a status marker. Possibly something entirely different that hasn't emerged yet. But the current trajectory can't continue because it's producing diminishing returns: more complexity, more conflict, more performance, less change. The people most committed to justice are starting to recognize that identity politics as status competition might feel righteous. Still, it doesn't build power, doesn't redistribute resources, doesn't change institutions, and doesn't create the material improvements in people's lives that supposedly justified the whole project. When the performance stops delivering even the feeling of progress, it becomes just another exhausting obligation that people fulfill because opting out carries social costs they can't afford to pay. That's not politics. That's just keeping up appearances in a game nobody's winning.

## Chapter 4: The Weaponization of Language: Belonging and Control

Language doesn't merely describe power, it exercises it. The words we're permitted to use, the phrases that signal insider status, the terminology that separates the initiated from the ignorant: these aren't neutral tools for communication. They're gates that open for some and lock for others. They're codes that grant access to communities, careers, and social capital. They're weapons that wound through exclusion as effectively as any slur wounds through attack. What's happened over the past decade isn't that progressive movements developed a more precise vocabulary to describe oppression. It's that language itself became the primary mechanism through which social hierarchies get enforced, in-groups protect their boundaries, and moral authority gets claimed and revoked. The expansion of terminology wasn't about clarity; it was about creating a constantly shifting landscape where only those with sufficient time, education, and social positioning could keep pace. The rest get left behind, marked as dinosaurs or bigots, not because they oppose justice, but because they failed to memorize this month's approved lexicon.

Consider what happens when a new term enters circulation. Someone coined "Latinx" as a gender-neutral alternative to "Latino" or "Latina." Within certain educated, politically progressive circles, adoption happens rapidly. Within months, using "Latinx" becomes a shibboleth, the word that distinguishes those who understand contemporary gender politics from those who don't. Publications update their style guides. Universities mandate their use in official communications. Conference presentations that fail to use it face criticism. But here's what nobody wants to acknowledge: the vast majority of people the term supposedly serves never adopted it. Polling consistently shows that only a tiny fraction of Hispanic/Latino Americans use "Latinx" to describe themselves, with many actively disliking the term. Yet the linguistic elite, academics, journalists, HR professionals, and activists continue using it, not because the affected community requested it, but because using it signals membership in the class that decides these things. The term doesn't serve the people it describes; it serves the people who describe them. It marks who possesses the cultural sophistication to stay current with linguistic fashion, and who doesn't.

This dynamic, terms adopted not for communicative utility but for status signaling, repeats across dozens of evolving vocabularies. The proliferation of initialism strings provides a perfect case study. LGBTQ became LGBTQIA, then LGBTQIA+, with some variants extending to LGBTQQIP2SAA. Each addition serves a valid purpose: acknowledging previously unnamed experiences, including marginalized groups within marginalized groups. But each addition also serves another purpose: raising the barrier to entry for participation in the conversation. If you can't remember whether the current standard is LGBTQ+ or LGBTQIA+ or something longer, you've marked yourself as outside the community of people who care enough to stay updated. Your confusion becomes evidence of your lack of commitment. The expansion doesn't improve precision; most people can't define the distinctions between all the letters, even as they dutifully recite them. The expansion performs a different function: it creates a moving target that only the sufficiently dedicated can track.

## The Purity Spiral Mechanics

The acceleration of linguistic change follows predictable mechanics, which sociologists call "purity spirals." When a community defines itself through moral superiority, we're the people who understand justice, who see what others miss, who stand on the right side of history, it faces a continuous problem: how do members demonstrate they're more committed than others? In traditional religious communities, this manifested through increasingly strict behavioral codes. In progressive spaces, it manifests through increasingly complex and rapidly changing language requirements. The member who adopts new terminology first, who corrects others' outdated usage, who coins novel distinctions that others hadn't considered, that member claims status. But once a term becomes widely adopted, it loses its status value. Everyone's saying "Latinx" now, so the early adopters need new vocabulary to distinguish themselves. They pivot to "Latine," or they abandon the project entirely and shift focus to some other linguistic frontier where they can again claim pioneer status.

This creates an exhausting treadmill where the point isn't arriving at better communication but continuously moving toward new linguistic territory. The exhaustion serves a purpose. People with demanding jobs, people raising children, people managing aging parents, people working multiple shifts, they can't keep pace. They lack the time to read the theory, follow the discourse, attend the workshops, and integrate the updates into their active vocabulary. Their inability to keep current doesn't reflect their values; it reflects their constraints. But in the purity spiral logic, falling behind with language equals falling behind morally. Your continued use of outdated terms, even terms that were mandatory last year, marks you as backward, as someone who stopped caring, as someone whose politics deserve suspicion. The treadmill isn't a bug; it's a feature. It ensures that only people with certain class advantages, education, leisure time, and immersion in elite institutions can maintain good standing. Everyone else gets perpetually marked as needing education, correction, or exclusion.

The spiral mechanics explain why so much energy gets devoted to policing language rather than changing material conditions. Correcting someone's terminology provides immediate, visible proof of your own superior understanding. It costs nothing, requires no sacrifice, and demands no engagement with complex policy questions or difficult tradeoffs. It's performative activism at its purest: maximum display of virtue, zero impact on power structures. When a progressive nonprofit spends staff meeting time debating whether to use "unhoused" or "homeless" or "housing-insecure," they're not advancing housing policy. They're engaging in status competition within the organization, establishing who possesses the most refined sensitivity, the most current awareness, the most sophisticated analysis. The debate serves internal hierarchy maintenance, not external impact.

## Vocabulary as Violence

Perhaps the most consequential development in language weaponization has been the expansion of harm into speech itself. Not speech that incites violence or creates hostile environments, that's traditional doctrine covered by existing law and policy. But the idea that using wrong terminology inflicts direct violence, that misgendering someone equals assault, that outdated language creates trauma equivalent to physical harm. This represents a category shift in how language gets understood, and the implications deserve scrutiny because they reveal how linguistic control masquerades as care.

The move works through strategic ambiguity about what "harm" means. Physical harm carries a clear definition: actions that damage the body or threaten its integrity. Psychological harm proves more difficult to define and measure, but still connects to clinically recognized conditions like PTSD, depression, or anxiety disorders. But the contemporary usage of harm in progressive spaces stretches far beyond either definition. Harm becomes anything that creates discomfort, anything that challenges someone's self-conception, anything that forces confrontation with perspectives they'd rather not consider. A speaker invited to campus whose views offend students: that presence causes harm requiring cancellation. A colleague who forgets someone's pronouns: that mistake causes harm requiring consequences. A professor who assigns historical texts containing racial slurs: that assignment causes harm requiring censorship. The elastic definition of harm means anyone can claim it, and once claimed, the claim becomes unchallengeable. Who are you to say what harms me?

This weaponization of harm language serves obvious purposes. It transforms disagreement into abuse, critique into attack, and discomfort into trauma. It places the person claiming harm in an untouchable position; you can't question their experience without committing additional harm. It inverts traditional power dynamics: the person most fragile, most easily wounded, most prone to claim injury gains most power in the interaction. But notice what gets lost: the distinction between actual violence and metaphorical violence, between material harm and emotional discomfort, between danger and disagreement. When everything becomes violence, nothing is. When all harm is treated as equivalent, we lose the ability to calibrate responses appropriately. The student who gets misgendered in class faces the same conceptual category as the student who gets physically assaulted. The vocabulary collapses meaningful distinctions, which means we can't think clearly about what actually matters.

The harm framework also creates perfect conditions for linguistic control. If using certain words causes harm, and causing harm equals committing violence, then preventing people from using those words becomes protecting safety. The controller isn't censoring speech; they're preventing assault. This framing appears throughout content moderation policies, corporate speech codes, and institutional guidelines. The language of harm transforms what's actually happening, powerful institutions limiting what ideas can be expressed, who can express them, and what consequences follow deviation, into something that sounds like compassion. We're not silencing you; we're protecting vulnerable people from your violence. The question of whether the claimed harm actually manifests in measurable ways never gets asked, because asking would itself constitute harm.

## The Professional Gatekeeping Function

The linguistic complexity serves another crucial function: professional gatekeeping. Certain career paths now require facility with specialized progressive vocabulary as a prerequisite for entry. Academia, journalism, corporate diversity and inclusion roles, nonprofit management, publishing, entertainment, tech company culture teams, these fields demand not just familiarity with the terms but skillful deployment that demonstrates ideological alignment. The vocabulary functions like a professional licensing exam, except the standards keep changing, and no official study guide exists. You learn through immersion in the right networks, the right educational institutions, and the right social media communities, which means you know if you have access to those spaces.

This creates a perfect class filter disguised as a moral filter. The child of educated professionals who attended elite colleges has spent years absorbing this vocabulary through ambient exposure. They've written papers using the terms, discussed them in seminars, and seen them deployed by professors and peers. When they enter the professional world, using terms like "intersectionality," "centering marginalized voices," "decolonizing practice," or "doing the work" comes naturally. They signal fluency effortlessly. The child of working-class parents who attended community college and state universities, even if they hold identical political values, lacks that ambient exposure. They're more likely to stumble over terminology, to use outdated phrasing, to seem less sophisticated even when making substantively similar points. The vocabulary disadvantages them not because they care less about justice, but because they lack the class markers that fluency signals.

The gatekeeping extends beyond initial hiring into ongoing career advancement. Organizations increasingly mandate training on proper terminology, often delivered by consultants charging premium rates to teach employees the current approved vocabulary. Employees who fail to adopt new terms quickly enough, who ask questions that suggest skepticism, or who seem insufficiently enthusiastic about linguistic updates, are marked as potential problems. Not problems in their actual job performance, but issues in their cultural fit, their values alignment, and their commitment to institutional priorities. The linguistic requirements serve what they've always served throughout history: separating those who belong from those who don't, identifying who possesses the right background and education to deserve their position, maintaining hierarchy while claiming to dismantle it.

Watch what happens when someone from outside the professional-managerial class challenges the vocabulary. When a working-class activist argues that all this language complexity alienates the communities supposedly being served, they're told they need to educate themselves, that their discomfort reflects internalized oppression, that their resistance demonstrates why the linguistic work matters so much. When union organizers point out that shop floor workers don't talk like this and won't respond to appeals framed in academic terminology, they're accused of making excuses for bigotry or coddling backward attitudes. The linguistic elite never considers that maybe their vocabulary actually impedes communication, that perhaps it serves their interests rather than the movement's goals, that maybe the working-class critics understand something about building broad coalitions that the college-educated activists have forgotten. The vocabulary protects itself. Any challenge to its utility gets reframed as a challenge to justice itself.

## Control Through Constant Instability

The final weapon isn't the complexity of the vocabulary; it's the instability. If the terms stayed constant, people could learn them. The barrier would be high but surmountable. Instead, the terms change constantly, often arbitrarily, sometimes reversing entirely. This creates a state of permanent uncertainty where nobody can be confident they're using language correctly. That uncertainty is the point. It keeps everyone off-balance, always vulnerable to correction, perpetually dependent on those who claim authority to dictate current usage.

Consider the term "people of color." For years, progressive spaces insisted on this phrasing over alternatives. It centered the humanity of the people described, avoided outdated terms, and provided an inclusive umbrella. But recently, some activists have argued that "people of color" is itself problematic; it centers whiteness by defining everyone in relation to white people, it flattens diverse experiences into a monolithic category, and it echoes earlier euphemisms with troubling histories. The new preferred term might be "BIPOC" (Black, Indigenous, and People of Color), except that term faces criticism for implying hierarchy among marginalized groups, or maybe the preference is moving back to specific ethnic identifications rather than umbrella terms at all. The point is: there's no stable answer. Whatever term you use, someone can argue it's wrong. Whatever phrasing you adopt, you're vulnerable to correction from someone claiming greater awareness.

This instability creates dependence. If you can't trust your own judgment about language, you need experts to guide you. Consultants who run training sessions. Activists who police discourse. Administrators who update institutional policies. These people gain power not from settling questions but from keeping questions perpetually unsettled. The moment consensus forms around proper usage, its authority weakens. If everyone knows the right terms, nobody needs the experts. So the experts have an incentive to maintain uncertainty, to keep discovering problems with current language, to keep advocating for new frameworks that require new vocabulary that requires new training that requires paying them to deliver it. The instability isn't a failure of the system. It's how the system perpetuates itself.

The people most harmed by this linguistic weaponization aren't the reactionaries who reject the premise entirely. They've opted out. They'll use whatever language they want and accept the social costs. The people most harmed are those who genuinely care about justice, who want to communicate respectfully, who try to stay current with terminology, but who can't keep pace with the acceleration. They're perpetually one term behind, perpetually anxious about offending, perpetually vulnerable to being marked as insufficiently committed. They spend mental energy tracking vocabulary that could go toward understanding policy, building coalitions, or taking action that matters. They get sorted out of spaces where they might contribute meaningfully, not because of their values or competence, but because they failed a linguistic test designed to be unpassable for anyone outside the elite class that writes the test.

Language should serve communication. When language serves control instead, when vocabulary becomes a weapon wielded to establish hierarchy, police boundaries, and maintain power, we've betrayed the purpose of words. What's been built isn't a more precise way to discuss justice.

It's a more sophisticated mechanism for deciding who gets to participate in those discussions and who gets locked out.

## The Dialect Trap

Here's what rarely gets discussed: the progressive linguistic revolution hasn't created a universal language of justice. It's made a class dialect. The vocabulary functions exactly like the accent that marks someone as educated or provincial, the pronunciation that reveals which side of the tracks you grew up on. Except this dialect pretends it isn't one. It claims to be simply "correct" language, the way educated people used to claim their grammar was "proper" while dismissing working-class speech patterns as corruption, the same dynamic, different words.

Listen to how foundation program officers talk versus the community organizers they fund. The program officer discusses "centering lived experience," "dismantling white supremacy culture," and "building intersectional praxis." The organizer talks about getting people what they need, fighting for their neighborhood, and making sure families can survive, with the same goals, in different languages. But only one language unlocks foundation funding. Only one vocabulary gets recognized as sophisticated enough for the grant proposal, the board presentation, and the conference panel. The organizer either learns to code-switch, performing the dialect that signals credibility to funders while speaking differently to their community, or they get cut off from resources. The dialect becomes a tax on working-class activists: translate your work into our language, or stay small.

The cruelty is that this linguistic barrier gets framed as progress. We're teaching people more evolved ways to talk about oppression. Never mind that the people experiencing oppression most directly often reject the vocabulary. Never mind that the complexity makes coalition-building harder, not easier. Never mind that movements with actual transformative power, labor organizing in the 1930s, civil rights activism in the 1960s, used language that deliberately prioritized accessibility over sophistication. They wanted everyone to understand. The contemporary progressive movement wants everyone to study.

Watch what happens when someone with the wrong dialect tries to join the conversation. A working-class woman at a community meeting talks about the "crazy" bureaucracy blocking her disability claim. Someone corrects her: That's ableist language, we don't use 'crazy' to describe systems. She apologizes, tries again: the "really messed up" bureaucracy. Another correction: let's use precise language. What specific mechanisms create barriers? She's trying to describe how she can't feed her kids because paperwork got lost, and she's getting a language lesson. The correction isn't helping her.

It's helping the correctors feel righteous. And it's teaching her that this space isn't for people who talk like her.

## Chapter 5: Social Justice as Branding: When Causes Become Commodities

The Nike swoosh appeared next to Colin Kaepernick's face with the tagline "Believe in something. Even if it means sacrificing everything." The campaign generated approximately $6 billion in brand value within months of launch. Nike sacrificed nothing. The company continued manufacturing shoes in Vietnamese factories where workers earned roughly $177 per month, less than half of Vietnam's living wage. The juxtaposition reveals everything you need to understand about social justice as branding: corporations discovered they could monetize the aesthetic of resistance while maintaining the economic structures that create the injustices being protested. The activism became the product. The outrage became the marketing strategy. And the audience, believing they were supporting radical change, became consumers purchasing the simulation of their own values.

This transformation, from social movements that threatened corporate power to corporate campaigns that simulate social movements, represents perhaps the most successful co-optation in capitalist history. It didn't happen through suppression or censorship. It happened through a more elegant mechanism: absorption and repackaging. Corporations studied the language, symbols, and emotional registers of social justice movements, then deployed them as brand differentiation strategies. What made this co-optation so effective is that it required no actual commitment to the underlying principles. A company could champion racial justice in its advertising while maintaining racially stratified pay structures internally. It could celebrate LGBTQ pride while donating to politicians who opposed LGBTQ protections. It could declare solidarity with workers while union-busting behind closed doors. The brand performance and the operational reality existed in separate spheres, and the market revealed something uncomfortable: most consumers didn't actually care about the gap.

## The Corporate Discovery

The breakthrough moment came when marketing departments realized that younger consumers, particularly millennials and Gen Z, made purchasing decisions based partly on perceived corporate values. Traditional brand loyalty centered on product quality, price, or status signaling. But research showed emerging consumers wanted brands that "stood for something," that "shared their values," that "made a difference." This created an obvious arbitrage opportunity: values are cheaper than quality. Improving product quality requires investment in materials, labor, and manufacturing. Improving product perception requires investment in messaging. If consumers would pay premium prices for brands that performed social consciousness, then the ROI on performative politics would dwarf the ROI on actual operational changes.

The pharmaceutical industry provides the clearest case study because its product outcomes are measurable. In 2020, numerous pharmaceutical companies released statements supporting Black Lives Matter, with elaborate commitments to racial equity. Johnson & Johnson pledged $100 million to advance racial justice. These announcements generated positive press and social media engagement. Meanwhile, the actual business of these companies, pricing medications, conducting clinical trials, and marketing drugs, remained unchanged in ways that disproportionately harm the communities they claimed to support. Black Americans remain dramatically underrepresented in clinical trials, meaning medications get tested primarily on white populations and then prescribed to everyone. Insulin prices, which disproportionately impact Black and Latino communities with higher diabetes rates, continued climbing. The commitment to racial justice operated exclusively in the communications department, never reaching R&D, pricing strategy, or trial recruitment.

What makes this particularly insidious is that the branding often makes material organizing harder. When Johnson & Johnson announces its racial justice commitment, activists trying to pressure the company on actual policies face a new obstacle: the company can point to its statement, its diversity initiatives, and its charitable contributions. The brand performance creates a shield against substantive critique. Activists who continue pushing face accusations of being unreasonable or ungrateful. Look at everything the company is already doing! The symbolic gesture, designed to absorb and deflect pressure, succeeds precisely because it creates the appearance of responsiveness while preserving the freedom to maintain extractive practices. The performance pre-empts the demand.

The consulting industry weaponized this dynamic into a business model. Firms like McKinsey and Deloitte now offer "diversity and inclusion consulting," helping corporations develop DEI strategies, conduct equity audits, and implement anti-bias training. These services generate billions in revenue annually. Yet McKinsey, which presents itself as a DEI leader, has worked for ICE (Immigration and Customs Enforcement) during family separation policies, for authoritarian regimes with dismal human rights records, and for opioid manufacturers developing strategies to increase sales of addictive medications. The same firm that helps one client develop anti-racism training helps another client maximize profits from human suffering. This isn't hypocrisy in the traditional sense. It's a business model sophistication. McKinsey sells social justice as a service while remaining ideologically neutral about whether social justice should actually exist. The cause becomes a pure commodity, purchased by clients who want the brand benefits without operational constraints.

## The Authenticity Trap

This created a new game: authenticity performance. If consumers would reward brands that seemed genuinely committed to social justice, then the competitive advantage would go to companies that could simulate authenticity most convincingly. Entire strategies were developed around this challenge. Brands hired "chief diversity officers" and promoted them publicly while keeping them away from actual decision-making power. They featured diverse faces in advertising while maintaining homogeneous leadership teams. They released land acknowledgments recognizing Indigenous territories while continuing to extract resources from those territories. Each gesture was designed to pass the authenticity test, to look like a genuine commitment to audiences primed to be skeptical but ultimately willing to believe.

Ben & Jerry's mastered this performance better than perhaps any brand. The ice cream company built its identity around progressive activism, taking vocal stances on criminal justice reform, climate change, and racial equity. The activist positioning worked brilliantly as brand differentiation; consumers who wanted their dessert to come with a side of political virtue could choose Ben & Jerry's over competitors. But Ben & Jerry's is owned by Unilever, a multinational conglomerate that has faced repeated accusations of environmental destruction, exploitative labor practices, and tax avoidance. The ice cream subsidiary gets to maintain its activist brand while the parent company pursues profit maximization strategies that contradict everything the brand claims to stand for. Consumers buying Ben & Jerry's imagine they're supporting a small, values-driven company. They're actually enriching a global conglomerate that deploys activist aesthetics as a market segmentation strategy.

The trap extends beyond obvious corporate bad actors. Consider Patagonia, frequently cited as a model of authentic corporate activism. The company donates significant revenue to environmental causes, uses recycled materials, and has taken real business risks for conservation. This authenticity isn't fraudulent; Patagonia's founder genuinely appears committed to ecological protection. Yet even this best-case scenario reveals the limitations of social justice as branding. Patagonia's business model depends on selling expensive outdoor gear to affluent consumers. The environmental crisis isn't fundamentally a consumer choice problem; it's a production and policy problem. The majority of emissions come from industrial processes and energy systems that individual consumer choices don't touch. By framing environmentalism as something you demonstrate through purchasing premium products, even authentic corporate activism reinforces the logic that social change happens through consumer behavior rather than collective political action. The cause becomes another lifestyle brand, accessible primarily to those with disposable income to spend on virtue.

The most sophisticated brands realized they didn't need to actually change anything; they needed to appear to be on a journey toward change. This innovation transformed corporate social justice from static claims into narrative arcs. A company wouldn't promise it had solved racism or achieved sustainability. It would acknowledge past failures, commit to doing better, announce initiatives and goals, then provide regular updates on "progress." This approach immunized against critique: yes, we still have problems, but look at the trajectory! The journey narrative also generated infinite content opportunities. Each incremental step, hiring a new diversity consultant, reaching a modest representation goal, and launching an employee resource group, became a chance for positive press. The brand could milk years of goodwill from merely moving in the right direction, regardless of whether it ever reached a destination or whether the destination itself was meaningful.

## The Nonprofit-Corporate Complex

This corporate discovery enabled a parallel transformation in the nonprofit sector. Organizations originally founded to challenge corporate power realized they could generate more revenue by partnering with corporations than by fighting them. The mechanism was elegant: corporations needed credibility for their social justice branding, and nonprofits could provide that credibility in exchange for funding. A corporate foundation donates to a racial justice nonprofit, then uses that relationship in marketing: "We're proud to partner with [prestigious nonprofit] in the fight for equity." The nonprofit gets funding, the corporation receives authenticity-washing, and both parties benefit from the transaction. The only loser is the social movement itself, which sees its institutional representatives absorbed into the very power structures they ostensibly oppose.

Human Rights Campaign illustrates this dynamic perfectly. HRC is America's largest LGBTQ advocacy organization, and it runs a "Corporate Equality Index" that scores companies on LGBTQ-friendliness. Companies that score well receive public recognition and use that score in marketing. But the methodology for achieving a high score focuses heavily on internal policies, nondiscrimination clauses, employee resource groups, and health benefits. A company can score perfectly while its actual business practices harm LGBTQ communities. Amazon consistently scores 100 on HRC's index. Amazon also faces repeated accusations of warehouse conditions that endanger workers, many of whom are LGBTQ. The company aggressively fights unionization efforts that would improve conditions. But Amazon has excellent nondiscrimination policies, so HRC gives it top marks, and Amazon uses that score to present itself as an LGBTQ ally. The nonprofit provides credibility laundering, the corporation offers funding, and the substantive issues affecting LGBTQ workers remain unaddressed.

This isn't an isolated failure; it's the predictable outcome when nonprofits become dependent on corporate funding. An organization that needs corporate donations can't afford to seriously challenge corporate power. It must focus its advocacy on areas where corporate interests aren't threatened. This creates a filtering effect: the issues that make it onto the agenda are precisely those issues where companies can make cosmetic changes without touching fundamental business models. Representation in advertising? Great, that's pure marketing. Pride month celebrations? Perfect, no operational changes required. Challenging how companies structure wages, benefits, and working conditions? That's off the table, too risky to the funding relationship. Social justice becomes limited to the horizon of what corporate donors will tolerate, and nonprofits that originally existed to expand that horizon become mechanisms for policing it.

The most perverse version of this dynamic involves "cause marketing" campaigns where corporations sell products by promising to donate a portion of proceeds to charity. Buy this soap, and the company will donate to clean water initiatives.

Buy this clothing, and profits go to women's empowerment. These campaigns perform a magic trick: they transform consumption into activism. The consumer gets to feel virtuous while buying products they would have bought anyway. The corporation generates sales through charitable appeals while donating far less than it gains in revenue. And the cause becomes dependent on consumer spending rather than collective political action or policy change. The campaign might raise meaningful money, some certainly do, but it reinforces the frame that social change happens through individual consumer choices rather than through organized power-building. The cause becomes a sales promotion vehicle, the nonprofit becomes a marketing partner, and the fundamental systems generating inequality remain untouched because nobody involved has an incentive to threaten them.

## The Measurement Problem

The transformation of social justice into branding created an acute measurement crisis: how do you evaluate whether corporate commitments to equity, sustainability, or justice actually mean anything? Traditional business metrics don't apply; you can't measure "commitment to racial justice" the way you measure profit margins. This vacuum created an enormous opportunity for what academics call "metric gaming", designing metrics that create the appearance of progress without requiring meaningful change. Companies didn't need to solve problems; they needed to choose metrics that made it look like they were solving problems.

Diversity statistics became the primary currency of this performance, and for good reason: they're easy to count and create clear numerical targets. A company announces it will achieve X% representation of women in leadership by 2025, or Y% representation of racial minorities across the organization. These goals sound concrete and measurable. But they reveal nothing about power distribution, pay equity, or working conditions. A company can hit diversity targets while maintaining dramatic pay gaps between white and non-white employees. It can celebrate gender diversity while systematically promoting men over women at equivalent experience levels. It can showcase diverse leadership, while those leaders have no actual authority to shape the company's direction. The numbers provide plausible deniability, we've achieved our goals!, while the underlying dynamics of power and resource distribution remain unchanged.

Environmental metrics demonstrate even more sophisticated gaming. Companies announce carbon neutrality or net-zero commitments by specific dates. These commitments generate tremendous positive press. But the methodologies for calculating carbon footprints allow extensive creative accounting. A company can claim carbon neutrality by purchasing offsets, paying someone else to plant trees or preserve rainforest, while continuing to increase its actual emissions. The offset market itself is notoriously fraudulent, with many projects that would have happened anyway being sold as offsets, or forests being "protected" that weren't actually under threat. But the carbon-neutral claim gets the marketing value regardless of whether the underlying climate impact changed. The metric becomes decorative rather than diagnostic, designed to facilitate branding rather than measure reality.

The sophistication reaches its peak with ESG (Environmental, Social, and Governance) scores, which purport to measure corporate responsibility across multiple dimensions. Asset managers use ESG scores to market "socially responsible" investment funds to consumers who want their capital to support virtuous companies. Entire rating agencies exist to calculate ESG scores. But the methodologies are proprietary, inconsistent across rating agencies, and heavily weighted toward factors companies can easily manipulate. A company with excellent disclosure practices can score well on ESG metrics while its actual environmental impact is catastrophic. A company can score highly on the "social" dimension by having good HR policies, while its supply chain involves forced labor. The scores create the appearance of rigorous evaluation while providing cover for investment strategies that differ little from conventional approaches. ESG became a $35 trillion industry not because it effectively channels capital toward social good, but because it allows asset managers to charge higher fees for products that perform basically the same as their non-ESG equivalents.

The measurement problem ultimately reveals why social justice as branding can never threaten actual power structures: the metrics that make brands look good are precisely those metrics that require no fundamental change. If a measurement system forces meaningful resource redistribution or operational transformation, companies simply won't adopt it. Instead, they adopt metrics that allow them to report progress while maintaining the business models that generate the problems being measured. The measurement infrastructure becomes part of the performance rather than a constraint on it, and everyone involved has an incentive to preserve this arrangement. The rating agencies get paid for producing scores, the companies get marketing material, the investment managers get product differentiation, and the consumers get to feel good about where their money goes. The only thing that doesn't happen is an actual change in how economic power is distributed across society, because no party to this transaction has an incentive to force that outcome.

What we're left with is a system where social justice exists primarily as an aesthetic choice rather than a political commitment, a brand position rather than a challenge to power. Corporations discovered they could profit from appearing to care about justice without sacrificing any of the practices that generate injustice. Nonprofits discovered they could secure funding by authenticating corporate performances rather than challenging corporate power. Consumers discovered they could purchase the feeling of political engagement without the inconvenience of actual political organizing. And the metrics that supposedly hold everyone accountable were designed from the start to enable rather than constrain this performance. The causes became commodities, traded in markets where everyone's incentives aligned around maintaining the appearance of change while preserving the reality of extraction. The performance became so sophisticated that most participants genuinely believe they're pursuing justice even as the system they've built makes justice structurally impossible to achieve.

# Chapter 6: The Gamification of Empathy: Virtual Virtue and Real Consequences

Empathy wasn't always trackable. It operated in the unmeasured spaces, the moment you held someone's grief without needing others to witness it, the conversation that changed how you saw another person's life, the quiet shift in understanding that altered your behavior without requiring announcement. Then we built systems that measured engagement, rewarded visibility, and quantified emotional labor. What couldn't be counted stopped counting. What could be performed replaced what could only be felt. We created empathy as a game, complete with points, leaderboards, and strategies for winning, and we're now discovering what happens when genuine human connection gets subjected to optimization mechanics.

The transformation follows a pattern familiar from other digital domains. Wikipedia editors discovered that making numerous small edits earned more status than making fewer substantive contributions. YouTube creators learned that outrage performs better than nuance. Twitter rewarded the quickest take, not the most thoughtful one. In each case, the platform's measurement systems created incentives that degraded the quality of the thing being measured. The same mechanics now govern how we demonstrate care. Empathy has become a performance optimized for the platforms where it's displayed, and those platforms reward quantity over depth, speed over reflection, and visibility over impact. The result is an empathy economy where the most valuable emotional labor isn't the kind that actually helps anyone; it's the kind that generates the most compelling content.

## The Empathy Olympics and the Creation of Suffering Content

Watch what happens when tragedy strikes. A shooting, a natural disaster, a celebrity death, within hours, social media fills with empathy performances, each competing for attention in an increasingly crowded market. The posts follow predictable templates: "I'm devastated." "I have no words." "My heart breaks for..." "Sending love to..." These statements perform an emotional response rather than describe it. They announce feelings without processing them, advertise concern without directing it toward action. Most importantly, they arrive fast, because in the empathy economy, first responders capture more engagement than late arrivals. The person who posts their grief within the first hour after the news breaks earns more visibility than someone who takes time to actually feel something before performing it.

This speed imperative fundamentally changes the nature of emotional response. Historically, processing tragedy took time. You learned what happened, sat with the information, talked to people close to you, developed an understanding of what the event meant, and how it connected to broader patterns. Then, maybe, you took action, donated money, showed up to help, changed something about how you lived. The emotional processing preceded and informed the response. Now the response must precede the processing. You must immediately broadcast your feelings, and those feelings must match the approved emotional register. Nuance looks like callousness. A delayed response looks like indifference. Asking questions looks like denial. The platform rewards instant, intense, unambiguous emotional display, which means the empathy isn't real in any meaningful sense; it's a reactive performance optimized for social mechanics rather than reflective feeling that might lead to useful action.

The competition escalates predictably. Early adopters post simple statements of solidarity. As the template saturates, later performers need differentiation. They add personal connection: "As a parent, I..." "As someone who survived..." "As a member of this community..." They escalate emotional intensity: from "saddened" to "heartbroken" to "shattered" to "unable to function." They demonstrate their empathy through elaborate descriptions of their own suffering in response to others' suffering. The person in Ohio who never met the shooting victims in Colorado describes being "triggered" and "traumatized" by the news. The white suburbanite declares they "can't breathe" after reading about police violence. The college student announces they're "literally shaking" after learning about distant injustice. Each escalation serves the same purpose: distinguishing their empathy performance from the thousands of others competing for attention in the same feed. The original tragedy becomes raw material for manufacturing content about the content creator's emotional sophistication and moral sensitivity.

This creates perverse incentives around suffering itself. In a traditional moral economy, suffering was something to minimize. You helped people who hurt, worked to prevent conditions that caused pain, and built systems that reduced harm. In the gamified empathy economy, suffering becomes valuable content, not to the people experiencing it, but to the people performing empathy about it. This explains the otherwise baffling phenomenon of privileged individuals seeking out stories of suffering to broadcast their emotional responses. They scroll through trauma narratives, watch videos of violence, and read detailed accounts of abuse, not primarily to understand or help but to harvest material for their own empathy performances. The suffering person becomes a prop in someone else's virtue demonstration. Their pain matters insofar as it provides an opportunity for others to showcase sensitivity, awareness, and emotional range. We've created an economy where other people's trauma functions as content infrastructure for empathy entrepreneurs.

The measurements matter because they determine what gets produced. Social media platforms track engagement, likes, shares, comments, reactions, and these metrics become the scoreboard for the empathy game. A post expressing concern about local homeless populations might generate dozens of responses. A post about a photogenic tragedy with clear villains and victims might create thousands. A post announcing you're "taking a mental health break because the state of the world is too much" might make tens of thousands, because it centers you while signaling empathy fatigue as evidence of deep feeling. The metrics train users in what works, and what works is empathy performance that maximizes engagement rather than empathy practice that actually reduces suffering. A person could spend an hour volunteering at a shelter or an hour crafting the perfect social media post about homelessness. The latter generates measurably more social reward, so the system teaches people to choose posting over helping, performance over practice.

## Secondary Trauma as Status and the Professionalization of Feeling

The gamification of empathy created a new status category: the person who cares so much that others' suffering causes them measurable harm. This isn't about people who work directly with trauma, therapists, emergency responders, and social workers, whose exposure to others' pain creates genuine psychological cost. This is about people whose primary relationship to suffering is consuming content about it, then claiming that consumption injured them. The term for this is "secondary trauma" or "vicarious trauma," and its migration from clinical contexts describing professionals who work with traumatized clients to casual usage describing anyone who reads sad news represents another example of concepts getting weaponized for status competition.

Consider the mechanics. Person A experiences direct trauma, assault, discrimination, and violence. Person B, who has no direct connection to Person A, reads about Person A's expertise on social media. Person B then claims they're traumatized by reading about it. Person B now competes with Person A for sympathy, resources, and attention, despite having experienced only mediated exposure to content about trauma rather than trauma itself. In some cases, Person B's claims actually receive more validation than Person A's, because Person B performs their suffering more skillfully, speaks the therapeutic language more fluently, or positions their trauma in ways that generate more engagement. The system rewards performed emotional fragility over actual resilience, which means people develop an incentive to emphasize their psychological vulnerability rather than their strength.

This dynamic spawned an entire vocabulary and professional infrastructure around emotional labor and self-care as commodity goods. "Emotional labor" originated as a sociological concept describing work that requires managing feelings, flight attendants maintaining cheerfulness, healthcare workers projecting calm, and service employees performing deference. The term described uncompensated labor, despite being required, invisible work, and exhausting. Then it migrated to describe any emotional processing anyone does, ever, no matter how voluntary or minimal. Someone asks you how your day was: "I don't have the emotional labor to explain right now." A friend needs support during a crisis: "I need to preserve my emotional labor for myself." The concept meant to name exploitation became a tool for avoiding basic human reciprocity. Every feeling, every interaction, every moment of caring got reframed as costly labor that must be compensated, conserved, or refused.

The professionalization of self-care followed the same trajectory. Self-care originally described practices developed by Black feminists and disability activists, people whose survival required actively counteracting systems designed to break them. It meant political resistance through self-preservation. It meant saying "the system wants me destroyed, so maintaining my capacity to fight is a revolutionary act." Then, wellness industries discovered they could sell self-care as a consumer product. Self-care became face masks, bath bombs, vacations, therapy speak, anything you could buy or photograph. More insidiously, it became a justification for avoiding difficulty. Can't attend the protest because of "self-care." Can't have hard conversations because "protecting my peace." Can't maintain relationships that require effort because "I need to center myself." Self-care rhetoric transformed from a tool for sustained resistance into an excuse for narcissistic withdrawal, and the empathy economy rewarded this transformation because posts about your self-care routine generate more engagement than posts about unglamorous work helping others.

## The Measurement Trap and Empathy Theater

The metrics create a specific problem: they measure empathy performance while making empathy practice invisible. A financial donation to a charitable organization registers on a public leaderboard, so people donate in ways that maximize visibility, $100 to a trending GoFundMe with social media integration rather than $1000 to an established organization doing effective work without publicity infrastructure. A post declaring solidarity gets tracked through engagement; an hour spent mentoring someone who needs guidance generates no data. A profile picture overlay supporting the current cause gets counted; voting for policies that would actually help the people you claim to support remains private. The measurable consistently displaces the meaningful because humans optimize for whatever gets scored.

This trap explains why empathy theater flourishes while empathy practice atrophies. Companies discovered they can generate goodwill through empathy performances, CEO apologies, corporate solidarity statements, and employee resource groups, without changing operational practices that create the problems requiring empathy. Universities implement bias response teams and emotional support systems while maintaining admissions and employment practices that reproduce inequality. Individuals change their profile pictures, update their pronouns, and post land acknowledgments, while their actual behavior, who they hire, who they mentor, and who they build relationships with, remains unchanged. The performance satisfies the social requirement to demonstrate care while exempting the performer from actually doing anything difficult or costly. You accumulate empathy points through visible gestures while your material impact remains zero or negative.

The gaming intensifies because everyone's playing simultaneously, which means the empathy required for any given situation inflates based on competition. A friend experiencing hardship used to warrant a phone call, a visit, or some practical help. Now the appropriate response requires public posting, fundraiser promotion, ongoing updates demonstrating you're still thinking about it, and performative emotional displays proving your concern. If you don't perform your empathy publicly, did you really care? The private phone call doesn't count because nobody witnessed it. The quiet, practical help doesn't matter because it generated no engagement. You must broadcast your empathy for it to register as real, which means empathy stops being about the person suffering. It starts being about your audience's perception of your emotional performance. The person in crisis becomes a supporting character in your empathy showcase, and their actual needs become secondary to what makes compelling content.

## Real Consequences: When Gamified Empathy Meets Actual Need

The virtualization of empathy produces material consequences. Medical professionals report patients arriving with self-diagnoses harvested from TikTok, demanding treatments for conditions they don't have, describing symptoms that match trending mental health content rather than their experience. Therapists describe clients who can articulate elaborate trauma frameworks and therapeutic vocabulary while remaining unable to build basic relationships or handle minor setbacks. Teachers encounter students who claim they can't complete assignments because they're "triggered" by course material, "traumatized" by grades, or "unsafe" when encountering disagreement, not students who faced genuine abuse or discrimination, but students who learned that performing fragility generates accommodation and care.

This doesn't mean nobody experiences real trauma. It implies the empathy game incentivizes overstating harm, performing fragility, and competing for victim status because that's what the system rewards. Someone who experienced severe childhood abuse but developed resilience gets less empathy than someone who experienced minor discomfort but performs suffering skillfully. The person who quietly manages their mental health challenges receives less accommodation than the person who broadcasts every mood fluctuation as a crisis. The system selects for people who game it most effectively, which means people who actually need help often get displaced by people who need attention. The finite resource of societal empathy gets allocated based on performance skill rather than actual need, and those least equipped to perform, people dealing with real crisis, people from cultures that don't valorize emotional display, people focused on surviving rather than narrating their survival, lose.

The damage extends to how we prepare people for difficulty. A generation raised in the empathy game learned that the appropriate response to hardship is seeking external validation, broadcasting suffering, and demanding that others manage their feelings. They didn't know that humans possess resilience, that difficulty builds capacity, that discomfort precedes growth, that other people can't regulate your emotional states for you. They learned that suffering makes you special, that fragility earns you care, that the world must accommodate your feelings, and that anyone who causes discomfort commits violence. These lessons leave people psychologically brittle, unable to handle the baseline adversity that characterizes human existence, relationships ending, jobs rejecting you, people disagreeing with you, and life not centering on your needs. The empathy game promised it was protecting vulnerable people. It produced vulnerability in people who didn't start that way, because it taught them that fragility pays.

The question isn't whether we should feel empathy or care about suffering. The question is whether the systems we built to measure and reward empathy actually increase human welfare or just create new hierarchies and status competitions. The evidence suggests the latter. We now have more empathy performance than ever, more posts, more awareness campaigns, more solidarity statements, more therapeutic language, alongside decreasing social trust, increasing loneliness, declining mental health, and diminishing capacity for the unglamorous work of actually helping people. The empathy economy generates endless content about caring while making it harder to care effectively. It valorizes emotional display while atrophying emotional capacity. It rewards performing concern while punishing the quiet competence that actually reduces suffering. We built a game where the winning move looks like empathy but functions as its opposite, a system that harvests human pain as content, transforms caring into a commodity, and replaces mutual aid with mutual performance. The score goes up while the suffering continues, and everyone's too busy tracking their metrics to notice the substitution.

## The Empathy Audit and the Collapse of Grace

The metrics created another problem nobody anticipated: they made forgiveness obsolete. When empathy becomes trackable, so does its absence. Miss the expected response to tragedy, and your silence gets audited. Failing to post solidarity at the approved moment, people notice the gap. Your participation in the empathy economy becomes a permanent record, searchable and scoreable. Someone screenshots your timeline during the crisis. Where were you? What were you doing? Why weren't you performing care when everyone else was? The absence of empathy performance gets read as the presence of malice, and there's no statute of limitations on empathy debts.

This fundamentally alters how humans relate to each other's failures. Before the empathy game, people understood that you couldn't be everything to everyone, couldn't stay informed about every tragedy, and couldn't emotionally process all the world's suffering simultaneously. You were allowed finite attention, allowed to miss things, allowed to focus on what was in front of you. Grace existed. Now the platforms create an expectation of omniscient awareness and instantaneous response. You should have known. You should have posted. Your failure to show empathy for every designated tragedy reveals your true priorities, and those priorities indict you. The friend who didn't comment on your crisis post doesn't get the benefit of the doubt; maybe they're dealing with their own emergency, perhaps they're helping in private ways, or maybe they process support differently. They get blamed. The coworker who didn't add the ribbon to their profile must not care. The silence proves complicity.

This mechanism serves power in fascinating ways. When empathy becomes mandatory performance, it becomes enforceable. Groups police each other's emotional displays, demanding conformity to approved responses. Step outside the boundaries and face consequences, social exile, professional punishment, and public shaming. The system claims to increase compassion but actually increases social control. Everyone monitors everyone else's empathy metrics, reporting deviations, enforcing orthodoxy. You must feel the correct things about the proper issues in the correct sequence with the correct intensity, and you must prove it through approved performances, or you're marked as morally deficient. The empathy economy promised liberation through emotional authenticity. It delivered conformity through emotional surveillance.

Watch who benefits from this arrangement. Not the people actually suffering, they're still suffering, just now with an audience. Not the people performing empathy, they're exhausted from the mandatory emotional labor of caring about everything constantly. The beneficiaries are the platforms that monetize the engagement, the consultants who sell empathy training, the influencers who've mastered the performance, and the institutions that substitute empathy statements for structural change. The empathy economy creates jobs, drives engagement, and generates content, all while the measurable suffering it supposedly addresses remains constant or increases. We built an entire industry around performing care, and the industry's success depends on the perpetuation of the problems it claims to solve.

# Chapter 7: The Theatre of Virtue: Performance Over Principle

Virtue used to cost something. Sheltering an escaped enslaved person in 1855 meant risking prosecution under the Fugitive Slave Act. Refusing to ride segregated buses in 1955 meant walking miles to work, and facing arrest, and harboring draft resisters in 1968 meant federal charges. These weren't symbolic gestures; they were material sacrifices that carried legal, economic, and social penalties. The person acting virtuously bore costs that the person remaining complicit avoided. This asymmetry mattered. It separated those willing to sacrifice something real from those merely performing agreement with the right ideas. The cost structure filtered for commitment. It meant virtue signaled something authentic about character rather than something strategic about social positioning.

Now consider the contemporary equivalent. Someone tweets their support for a cause, adds a hashtag to their profile, or shares an infographic. These actions involve no sacrifice. They impose no cost. They require no courage. Yet they generate social rewards, likes, shares, follows, the warm internal glow of having "done something." The theatre of virtue operates on this inversion: maximum social credit for minimum actual commitment. The performance has completely detached from the principle it supposedly represents. What matters isn't whether you changed

2106

anything about how power operates in the world. What matters is whether you demonstrated, to the right audience, that you hold the correct positions. The demonstration has become the entirety of the ethical act.

This isn't about whether the causes are worthy; many are. It's about what happens when the primary work of social change shifts from confronting power to curating appearances. When the performance becomes more important than the outcome, when looking virtuous matters more than being effective, when the goal shifts from winning concrete improvements to maintaining unblemished moral credentials, the entire project corrupts. The theatre doesn't just fail to advance justice, it actively impedes it by replacing strategies that work with strategies that feel good.

## The Social Audit and the Permanent Record

Here's where the theatre gets interesting: it's developed accountability mechanisms that have nothing to do with whether your actions produced results and everything to do with whether your performance meets constantly evolving standards of ideological purity. Call it the social audit, the retrospective examination of everything you've ever said, posted, liked, or failed to denounce, searching for evidence that at some point you fell short of whatever the current standard happens to be.

The social audit operates on several disturbing principles. First, it assumes perfect knowledge is possible and mandatory. You should have known better, regardless of when the statement was made or what information was available at the time. A joke that was culturally acceptable in 2010 becomes evidence of moral failure when examined in 2025, even though the standards shifted and nobody consulted you about the change. The audit applies contemporary frameworks retroactively, treating your inability to anticipate future ideological developments as proof of deficient character rather than normal human limitation. This creates an impossible situation: you're expected to have always already known what you're only learning now, and your past ignorance convicts you of permanent ethical inadequacy.

Second, the audit treats all transgressions as equally disqualifying, because it's not actually interested in proportionality or growth or learning. It's interested in finding grounds for exclusion. Whether you used an outdated term once in 2008 or actively campaigned against civil rights legislation, the audit often produces similar outcomes: you're morally compromised, your opinions are suspect, your participation in conversations about justice is inappropriate. The lack of proportionality isn't a bug; it's the point. If the goal were actually encouraging growth and improvement, the system would distinguish between minor infractions and major betrayals, would recognize that people learn and change, and would offer paths toward redemption. Instead, the audit functions as a permanent surveillance mechanism that ensures everyone has an exploitable vulnerability. Everyone has said something that wouldn't pass current standards. Everyone has a liability in their past. This universal vulnerability is useful; it means anyone can be taken down whenever politically convenient.

Third, the audit never closes. You can't serve your time and move on because there's no statute of limitations and no forgiveness mechanism. The old statements remain permanently available, permanently weaponizable. Any moment, someone might excavate them and present them as evidence that you're not who you claim to be. This creates perpetual anxiety and perfect compliance incentives. You learn to police not just your current statements but your entire digital history, deleting anything that might be recontextualized as problematic. You learn to never commit to positions that might later become unfashionable. You know that the safest move is zealous enforcement of current orthodoxy, because the best defense against being audited is being the one conducting audits. The system produces informers, not reformers.

## Performative Allyship and the Extraction Economy

The theatre of virtue has created a particularly grotesque economic relationship disguised as solidarity: performative allyship, where privileged individuals extract social capital from others' oppression without contributing anything useful to addressing it. The mechanism is elegant in its parasitism. Someone identifies a marginalized group's struggle, learns the approved vocabulary, posts the right statements, shows up to the photogenic protests, and collects credit for being an ally, all while doing precisely nothing that would threaten their own position in the hierarchies that produce the marginalization they claim to oppose.

Watch how this works in practice. A wealthy white executive attends a protest against police violence, posts photos on Instagram with captions about "doing the work," and receives praise for "using their privilege to amplify marginalized voices." Has this person done anything to address police violence? Have they redirected any of their wealth toward organizations providing legal defense for arrested protesters? Have they used their professional network to pressure district attorneys about prosecutorial discretion? Have they sacrificed any comfort, security, or social standing? No. They've participated in political theatre, documented their participation, and collected social rewards for the performance. The extracted benefit flows toward the performer; the "amplification" they provided generated more visibility for themselves than for any marginalized person.

This extraction economy has created an entire industry. Diversity consultants who charge corporations five-figure fees to conduct "implicit bias training" that produces no measurable change in hiring or promotion patterns but allows executives to claim they've "addressed" workplace inequality. Authors who write books about checking your privilege that sell primarily to people who already agree and want their existing views validated. Speakers who command premium fees to tell audiences about oppression, while the people actually experiencing that oppression can't afford tickets to hear their own stories recounted. The money flows toward performers and away from material redistribution. The attention centers on the ally rather than those supposedly being helped. The entire apparatus exists to allow privileged people to feel good about themselves without surrendering any actual privilege.

The perverse genius of performative allyship is that it's structured to be uncriticizable from within its own logic. If someone from a marginalized group points out that an ally's performance isn't helping, that it's actually extractive or counterproductive, the ally can respond that the criticism proves they're "doing the work" effectively, because real allyship means "being uncomfortable" and "listening when you're called in." If nobody criticizes them, that proves they're getting it right. The system is unfalsifiable, which should immediately raise suspicion. Meanwhile, the actual work of material redistribution, union organizing, tenant organizing, mutual aid networks, and debt abolition languishes for lack of resources and attention, because it offers no opportunity for performance. You can't Instagram your way through a picket line negotiation. You can't tweet yourself into meaningful wealth redistribution. The stuff that works is boring, slow, unglamorous, and requires genuine sacrifice. The theatre remains popular precisely because it demands nothing real.

## The Confession Ritual and Public Flogging

The theatre of virtue has revived practices that looked archaic when we observed them in religious fundamentalism or authoritarian regimes: the public confession and the ritual denunciation. These ceremonies serve critical functions in maintaining ideological control, and studying their mechanics reveals how supposedly progressive movements have reconstructed the coercive dynamics they claim to oppose.

The confession follows a formula. Someone violates current norms, uses the wrong terminology, asks an unwelcome question, or fails to demonstrate sufficient enthusiasm for the latest cause. Criticism arrives swiftly, often disproportionate to the infraction. The violator has two options: resist and face escalating social costs, or confess. The confession must meet specific requirements. It must be abject, not "I made a mistake" but "I caused harm." It must be comprehensive, not "I used an outdated term" but "I'm examining all the ways my privilege has caused me to perpetuate systems of oppression." It must be gratifying to thank those who called you out for "educating" you. It must be permanent, committed to writing, publicly posted, and available for future reference.

Here's what the confession actually accomplishes: it extracts submission. The content matters less than the ritual performance of subordination. You demonstrate that you accept the authority of those judging you, that you recognize their right to define transgression and demand penance, that you'll comply with whatever standards they impose. The confession isn't about growth or learning; it's about establishing hierarchy. The person demanding confession is asserting dominance. The person confessing is accepting subordinate status. This is why the confessions are never sufficient on their own; there's always something more you should acknowledge, some deeper complicity you haven't examined, some additional work you need to do. The insufficiency is structural. If the confession were ever adequate, the hierarchy would collapse.

The public flogging that accompanies or follows confession serves its own purpose: demonstrating to observers what happens when you step out of line. The punishment isn't proportional to the offense because it's not actually about the offense; it's about maintaining compliance through fear. The person being flogged becomes an object lesson. Everyone watching learns what to avoid, what not to say, which questions not to ask, and which doubts not to express. The flogging is theater too, but not for the person being punished, for everyone else. It's a warning: this could be you. Comply, or face similar treatment.

What makes this especially effective is that the standards are deliberately ambiguous and constantly shifting. You can't simply learn the rules and follow them, because the rules change and nobody announces the changes until you've already violated them. This is called liquid moderation, keeping people perpetually off-balance, never quite sure whether what they're about to say crosses a line they can't see. The uncertainty itself produces compliance. When you don't know what's forbidden until after you've done it, the safest strategy is saying nothing at all, or only repeating what others have already said without consequence. The system successfully suppresses dissent not through brute force but through ambient anxiety about potential social consequences.

## The Illusion of Action and the Atrophy of Organizing

Perhaps the most damaging aspect of virtue theater is what it displaces: actual political organizing that might threaten power structures. The theater creates an illusion of action that's worse than inaction because it satisfies the urge to do something without accomplishing anything. This matters because human beings have finite time, energy, and attention. When those resources flow toward performative activities, they're not available for effective ones. The theater isn't just useless, it's actively harmful because it absorbs capacity that could go toward real organizing.

Consider the trajectory of progressive political energy over the past decade. Countless hours have been spent debating terminology, policing language, calling out problematic statements, canceling insufficiently pure allies, and curating social media profiles to display correct positions. Imagine redirecting that energy toward tenant organizing in cities where rent consumes sixty percent of working-class income. Toward building mutual aid networks that provide material support when state systems fail. Toward strategic litigation that challenges corporate consolidation. Toward voter registration and mobilization in districts where turnout determines representation. Toward strike support for workers confronting employers. These activities are difficult, time-consuming, and unglamorous. They require sustained commitment, tolerance for setbacks, and willingness to work alongside people who don't share your entire worldview. They produce incremental progress rather than viral moments. They're exactly the kind of work that actually redistributes power, which is precisely why they're less popular than posting your pronouns.

The theater has also corroded the skills necessary for effective organizing. Building a coalition requires finding common ground with people who differ from you, which means tolerating disagreement on some issues to advance agreement on others. It means prioritizing concrete goals over ideological purity. It means accepting that your allies might hold views you find objectionable on topics unrelated to your shared objective. The theater teaches exactly the opposite: treat any deviation from orthodoxy as disqualifying, refuse to collaborate with anyone who's expressed a problematic opinion, prioritize purity over effectiveness, and value symbolic victories over material ones. These habits don't build power; they fragment movements into ever-smaller factions, each convinced of its own righteousness and everyone else's inadequacy.

The atrophy shows in outcomes. Despite unprecedented visibility for progressive causes, despite the apparent cultural dominance of social justice language, material conditions for marginalized groups have worsened by many measures. Wealth inequality has increased. Housing costs have exploded. Real wages have stagnated. Incarceration rates remain obscene. Climate change accelerates. Police budgets grow. Unions represent a smaller percentage of workers than they have in a century. The theater has succeeded spectacularly at changing what corporations say in their marketing materials and what words are acceptable in institutional communications. It has failed at changing how resources and power actually distribute across society. That's not a coincidence; it's the predictable result of investing energy in performance rather than power-building.

The lesson here is uncomfortable but necessary: good intentions don't excuse counterproductive strategy. Feeling virtuous doesn't matter if your actions undermine the goals you claim to support. The theatre of virtue has become an obstacle to justice, not a path toward it. It allows privileged people to feel righteous without sacrificing privilege. It satisfies the psychological need to be "on the right side" without requiring the hard work of actually moving anyone to a better position. It creates the appearance of a movement while the actual infrastructure of organizing deteriorates from neglect. And it does all this while claiming moral superiority over anyone who points out that the performance isn't working.

The alternative isn't cynicism or abandoning the pursuit of justice; it's redirecting energy from theatre to power. It's building organizations rather than building social media followings. It's measuring success by outcomes rather than applause. It's accepting that progress comes from sustained effort on unglamorous work rather than perfect public statements. It's recognizing that virtue is what you do when nobody's watching, not what you perform when everyone is. The show must end before the work can begin.

## The Amnesia Machine and the Vanishing of History

Here's what the theatre of virtue does to institutional memory: it erases it. Not deliberately, that would require acknowledging that history exists in the first place. The erasure happens through a more insidious mechanism: the assumption that moral clarity only emerged recently, that previous generations were simply bigots who didn't know better, that all the complexity and strategic thinking and coalition-building that produced actual progress can be dismissed as hopelessly compromised by the moral failures of its time.

This is the amnesia machine at work. It looks at the past and sees only problems, never precedents worth studying. The civil rights movement? Sure, it ended legal segregation, but some of its leaders held views on gender or sexuality that wouldn't pass current standards, so what can we really learn from them? The labor movement? Built power for workers, yes, but it excluded various groups at various times, so its strategies are tainted. Second-wave feminism? Advanced women's rights dramatically, but failed to center certain identities, so it's more cautionary tale than instructive history. The pattern repeats: identify the moral imperfections of past movements using current standards, declare them insufficient, and proceed as if you're inventing political organizing from scratch.

This would merely be not very smart except for what it destroys: strategic knowledge. The movements that actually won things, that extracted concrete concessions from entrenched power, that built institutions capable of sustaining themselves across generations, that created leverage where none existed before, they learned through failure what works and what doesn't. That knowledge isn't written in manifestos. It's encoded in organizational practice, passed from experienced organizers to new ones, and refined through trial and error over decades. When you decide that everyone who came before was too problematic to learn from, you lose that knowledge. You end up reinventing wheels, repeating mistakes that were solved forty years ago, and getting outmaneuvered by power structures that have centuries of experience. At the same time, you're armed with nothing but moral certainty and a Twitter account.

The amnesia machine produces activists who can recite theory but can't run a meeting. Who understands intersectionality as an analytical framework but can't build a coalition that includes people with a high school education? Who can identify every problematic element in historical movements but can't organize their workplace? The knowledge of how to actually build and wield power atrophies because it's associated with people who weren't pure enough by contemporary standards. And power doesn't care about your purity. It cares whether you can challenge it effectively. Right now, you can't.

## Chapter 8: Navigating Moral Outrage as Social Currency

Moral outrage used to cost something. When abolitionists stood in town squares denouncing slavery, they risked violence. When war protesters burned draft cards, they faced prison sentences. When activists chained themselves to trees or occupied buildings, they accepted arrest records that would follow them for life. The outrage wasn't free; it extracted real prices from those who expressed it, which meant it functioned as a credible signal. You couldn't fake commitment when commitment required sacrifice. The filtering mechanism worked automatically: people who weren't serious about change didn't pay the freight needed to pursue it.

Then we built infrastructure that made outrage costless to express and profitable to perform. Social media platforms discovered that anger drives engagement more reliably than any other emotion. News organizations learned that outrage headlines generate more clicks than sober analysis. Content creators found that righteous fury attracts subscribers faster than thoughtful commentary. Universities and corporations developed entire departments dedicated to identifying and responding to expressed outrage. We constructed an economy where moral indignation became the most valuable currency you could mint, and the minting cost dropped to zero. Post a tweet. Record a video. Share an article with an outraged caption. The production costs nothing. The potential returns, attention, influence, opportunities, and status are enormous. We've created arbitrage conditions where anyone can buy outrageously cheap and sell it dear, and we're shocked that the market is flooded with supply.

The transformation isn't that people became more easily offended or that genuine injustices disappeared. It's that we changed the economic incentives around moral expression so dramatically that rational actors optimize for outrage production rather than problem-solving. This creates predictable distortions that undermine the very causes the outrage supposedly serves, because the behaviors that maximize outrage currency actively sabotage the work required to address underlying issues. Understanding these mechanics isn't cynicism; it's a prerequisite for anyone who wants to distinguish authentic moral clarity from profitable moral theater.

## The Outrage Inflation Cycle and Attention Scarcity

Economics teaches that when you dramatically increase the supply of any currency without a corresponding increase in what it can purchase, you get inflation. The currency's value degrades. What was bought in substantial quantities now buys less. This exact dynamic governs moral outrage in the attention economy. Ten years ago, expressing outrage over genuine injustice might command significant attention. The audience hadn't yet developed saturation fatigue. The performance was relatively novel. But as millions of people began expressing outrage daily, as platforms filled with performative anger, as every minor slight got framed as a moral catastrophe, the currency inflated. Each instance of expressed outrage now commands less attention than before, which means performers must escalate intensity to maintain returns.

Watch the progression. Initial outrage over police brutality expressed measured anger about systemic patterns. It drew attention and sparked productive conversations. As that format saturated, performers needed differentiation. Some adopted increasingly extreme rhetoric, not "this is unjust" but "this is genocide," not "we need reform" but "we must abolish everything." Others competed by finding new outrages; if police violence became familiar territory, they highlighted violence in other institutions, other contexts, other interactions, constantly expanding the definition of what constitutes sufficient provocation for moral fury. Still others differentiated through intensity of response, not "I'm angry" but "I'm literally shaking," not "this is wrong" but "I can't even," performing emotional fragility so extreme it justified any reaction. The escalation spiral feeds itself. As extreme responses become normalized, moderate expressions of concern register as insufficient. Proportionality disappears because proportional responses command no attention in an oversaturated market.

The attention scarcity driving this inflation operates on multiple levels. Platform algorithms reward engagement, and negative emotions generate more engagement than positive ones; anger gets shared more than contentment, and fear spreads faster than reassurance. But humans also face cognitive limitations. You can only process so many moral crises before you develop defense mechanisms. Psychologists call this "compassion fatigue" or "empathy burnout." Still, the economic frame is clearer: you're spending a limited resource, your capacity to care, and the demand on that resource keeps accelerating past your ability to supply it. When everything becomes an emergency, nothing remains an emergency. When every injustice demands your immediate fury, you stop being able to distinguish the urgent from the trivial. The market response is predictable: performers escalate intensity to break through your defenses, which accelerates your fatigue, which requires further escalation. The currency inflates because we're all chasing the same scarce resource, a human attention span that hasn't expanded despite exponential increases in claims upon it.

## Strategic Outrage and Career Advancement

Here's what nobody says out loud: expressing the right outrage at the right time has become a legitimate career strategy, particularly in knowledge work sectors, academia, media, and technology. Understanding this requires examining what outrage actually purchases in professional contexts. It purchases reputation as someone who "gets it", who understands contemporary social justice frameworks, who can navigate identity politics competently, and who won't create HR problems. It provides access to networks and opportunities available only to those who demonstrate proper political consciousness. It purchases insulation from criticism, because someone who loudly denounces injustice gains borrowed credibility that makes questioning their motives or methods appear suspect. Most importantly, it provides advancement in zero-sum competitions where anything that differentiates you from equivalently credentialed peers provides an advantage.

Consider how this operates in academic job markets, where hundreds of qualified candidates compete for a single position. Your dissertation quality, publication record, and teaching evaluations matter, but dozens of candidates will have comparable credentials. What distinguishes you? One effective strategy: demonstrate that your work advances social justice goals, that you can teach from frameworks emphasizing systemic oppression, that you'll contribute to diversity initiatives, and express appropriate outrage over institutional failings. This isn't deception; many candidates genuinely hold these commitments. But the market creates pressure where even those without such commitments face incentives to perform them convincingly, because doing so provides a competitive advantage over candidates who focus solely on scholarly merit. The outrage becomes capital you invest for professional returns.

The same dynamics operate in corporate environments, particularly within companies that have embraced diversity, equity, and inclusion frameworks. Being the person who identifies problematic language in company communications, who points out representation gaps in marketing materials, and who expresses concern about bias in hiring practices, these actions generate visibility and establish your identity as someone attuned to social justice issues. They signal alignment with stated corporate values. They demonstrate awareness that distinguishes you from colleagues who just do their jobs without noticing political dimensions. In organizations where leadership has committed to DEI goals, being seen as a contributor to those goals creates opportunity. You get invited to task forces and committees. You gain access to executives. You establish a reputation that protects you in performance reviews, because managers fear that criticism of someone known for social justice advocacy might be interpreted as retaliation for speaking up. The outrage functions as a strategic investment with calculable returns.

This professionalization of outrage creates severe selection effects. The people most incentivized to express it aren't those most affected by injustice; they're those positioned to convert moral expression into career capital. A tenured professor who already has security can afford authentic outrage that might offend colleagues. A graduate student dependent on recommendation letters faces different calculations. A corporate employee whose manager opposes DEI initiatives takes career risks by expressing outrage that someone whose manager champions such initiatives doesn't face. The result: outrage expression concentrates among those with either enough security that costs don't matter or enough strategic sophistication to recognize that apparent costs are actually investments. The people for whom injustices aren't abstract theories but lived experiences often can't afford the performance required to convert those experiences into professional advancement, because they're busy surviving the actual conditions others are performing outrage about.

## The Outrage Audit and Social Credit Systems

We've developed informal but remarkably sophisticated systems for tracking who expresses appropriate outrage with sufficient enthusiasm at required moments. Miss too many opportunities to perform outrage, and you accumulate a deficit in social credit. Fail to express outrage over the designated outrage-worthy event, and people notice the silence. Express outrage at the wrong intensity; too much suggests performative excess, too little suggests insufficient commitment, and you get coded as unreliable. These audit mechanisms don't operate through formal tracking, but the accounting happens nonetheless. People remember who showed up, who stayed silent, and who said the right things when it mattered.

The audit operates most intensely within professional and social communities that define themselves through progressive political identity. Academic departments, activist organizations, cultural institutions, creative industries, anywhere moral positioning substitutes for organizational purpose, you'll find elaborate outrage accounting. When a scandal breaks, when an injustice gets exposed, when a controversy erupts, community members face immediate pressure to declare their positions. The declaration format follows predictable templates: "I'm devastated to learn..." "I stand with..." "We must do better..." The content matters less than the timing and visibility. Post quickly, post publicly, post emphatically. Your social credit score depends on demonstrating that you recognized the moment as outrage-worthy and responded appropriately.

The credit system creates absurd situations where people who've done nothing wrong and contributed nothing helpful nonetheless gain credit simply for expressing correct outrage, while people actually working on solutions get audited for insufficient performative fury. Imagine a nonprofit director who's spent twenty years building job training programs in underserved communities. He measures success in lives changed, families stabilized, and communities strengthened. Now imagine a graduate student who tweets prolifically about systemic racism and shares infographics about inequality. When controversy strikes, the graduate student gains social credit for immediately posting outraged condemnation. The nonprofit director, busy with actual work, posts nothing. According to the audit mechanics, the graduate student performed better. The social credit system rewards performance over production, declaration over demonstration, outrage expression over outcome generation. It inverts merit by assigning value to symbolic gestures while ignoring substantive contribution.

These credit systems also enable manipulation through what economists call "moral licensing." Express sufficient outrage about distant injustices, and you purchase a license to ignore proximate ones. A professor who loudly denounces racial inequality in public statements but runs a lab with a discriminatory culture has banked enough outrage credit that colleagues hesitate to question the contradiction. A corporation that posts elaborate solidarity statements after police shootings but maintains exploitative labor practices in supply chains has purchased moral cover through symbolic outrage. The more extreme your expressed outrage over abstract injustices, the more insulation you gain against scrutiny of your concrete practices. The currency functions as an indulgence purchase; buy enough outrage credits, and you're absolved of actual moral obligation.

## The Exhaustion Trap and Tactical Deployment

The relentless demand for outrage expression creates a psychological trap: you must remain perpetually activated, continuously furious, always ready to demonstrate appropriate moral response to the latest injustice. This requirement conflicts with basic human psychological capacity. Nobody can sustain genuine outrage indefinitely. Real anger exhausts itself; it spikes in response to provocation, drives action, then subsides as you either address the problem or accept you can't. But the social credit system demands permanent activation. You can't say, "I've expressed all the outrage I'm capable of producing; I need emotional rest." That reads as moral failure. You can't say, "I'm conserving my outrage for issues I can actually influence." That reads as insufficient commitment. You're required to perform inexhaustible fury, which means you're required to fake it.

The exhaustion trap produces several pathological adaptations. Some people develop outrage personas, performative identities they inhabit online or in political contexts that don't reflect their actual emotional states. They learn to generate outraged content the way shift workers clock in, it's production, not passion. Others develop outrage addiction, where the social rewards of performance train them to seek provocations that justify expressing fury. They begin experiencing genuine anger in response to stimuli that wouldn't have bothered them before the reinforcement schedule established anger as a profitable response. Still others burn out entirely, withdrawing from political engagement because the demands exceeded their psychological capacity. None of these adaptations serves justice. The personas are fake. The people with an addiction are unreliable. The burned-out are absent. But the system demands continuous performance regardless of human limitations.

Sophisticated actors recognize these dynamics and deploy outrage tactically rather than authentically. They understand outrage as a tool you use strategically rather than an emotion you experience genuinely. Watch how activist organizations operate: they manufacture outrage campaigns by identifying targets, developing narratives, coordinating messaging, and timing releases for maximum impact. This isn't a spontaneous moral response to injustice; it's a planned tactical deployment of outrage as a weapon. The goal isn't expressing genuine feelings but generating specific effects: pressure on institutions, media attention, resource extraction from targets, and reputation damage to opponents. The manufactured outrage may serve legitimate purposes, but pretending it's authentic emotion rather than tactical calculation obscures what's actually happening. You're watching strategic communication designed to manipulate public sentiment, not witnessing a genuine moral witness.

This tactical dimension explains otherwise puzzling patterns. Why does outrage over certain issues spike and crash on predictable cycles rather than tracking with actual severity? Because organizers are deploying attention strategically, concentrating pressure when it serves purposes, letting issues fade when they don't. Why do some injustices generate sustained fury while others get ignored despite being objectively worse? Because the outrage market responds to what's useful, not what's urgent. Why does expressed outrage often correlate inversely with willingness to make personal sacrifices addressing the problem? Because the outrage is performance designed to extract concessions from others, not authentic commitment driving self-sacrifice. Recognizing these patterns doesn't mean the injustices aren't real or the outrage isn't sometimes justified. It means understanding that much of what presents as spontaneous moral response is actually calculated deployment of outrage as social currency, spent strategically by people who understand the exchange rates.

The most sophisticated operators hoard their outrage, deploying it selectively when doing so purchases maximum advantage. They recognize that constant outrage inflation makes each expression worth less, so they conserve their currency for moments when spending it generates optimal returns. They also acknowledge that being the person who identifies the outrage-worthy issue before others provides a first-mover advantage, and you establish yourself as a moral authority who recognized the problem early. This creates perverse incentives to search for new injustices, new frameworks for interpreting existing conditions as outrageous, and new frontiers where your moral clarity distinguishes you from those still operating under old paradigms. The market rewards discovery, which means the supply of identified outrages expands faster than the supply of actual injustices, because people are incentivized to find provocations that justify deploying their currency.

## Breaking the Currency: Outrage Inflation Endgame

Every inflated currency eventually faces reckoning. When everyone holds an abundant supply of something that purchases less and less, the market corrects. Sometimes, through a crash, the currency becomes worthless, trust collapses, and systems break. Sometimes, through reformation, new mechanisms emerge that restore scarcity and value. Sometimes, through replacement, people abandon the degraded currency and adopt alternatives. The moral outrage economy approaches similar inflection points, though which correction mechanism will dominate remains unclear.

The crash scenario looks like what psychologists call "emotional blunting"; populations simply stop responding to outrage altogether. The constant assault of performed fury, the endless demands for emotional response, the inflation that made each expression meaningless, eventually, people's psychological defenses overwhelm their capacity to care. They develop calluses. They stop engaging with moral claims entirely because distinguishing authentic from performed has become impossible, and the cognitive load of constant evaluation exceeds the benefit. This collapse would be catastrophic for actual justice work, because it would mean losing the capacity to mobilize people around genuine injustices. The performers crying wolf would have so thoroughly exhausted the audience that real wolves would have been ignored. Some evidence suggests this is already happening among younger cohorts who've lived their entire adult lives in saturated outrage environments and are developing resistance.

The reformation scenario involves developing new mechanisms that restore meaning to moral expression by reintroducing cost structures that filter for authentic commitment. This might mean communities developing reputations for following through on expressed commitments. If you express outrage about an issue, you're expected to actually work on addressing it, and failure to do so damages your credibility. It might mean standards that distinguish between symbolic gestures and substantive action, reserving status recognition for the latter. It might mean rebuilding norms around proportionality, where the intensity of expressed outrage needs to match the severity of the injustice rather than the strategic benefit of escalation. These reforms would require collective will to stop rewarding performative outrage and start demanding actual sacrifice, which faces obvious collective action problems. Everyone benefits from deflating the currency, but each benefits most from being the last person to stop inflating it.

The replacement scenario is perhaps most interesting: people might abandon outrage altogether as moral currency and adopt alternative frameworks that can't be gamed through performance. What would those look like? Possibly systems that measure outcomes rather than expressions, judging people's commitment to justice by what they accomplished rather than what they proclaimed. Perhaps frameworks that emphasize humility over certainty, recognizing that complex social problems require experimentation and tolerance for uncertainty rather than performative conviction. Possibly approaches that value concrete help over abstract solidarity, where showing up and doing unglamorous work matters more than broadcasting correct opinions. These alternatives exist in small-scale communities and organizations that have consciously rejected outrage currency, but scaling them requires solving difficult coordination problems about how we recognize and reward moral commitment without creating new exploitable performance opportunities.

None of these futures is inevitable. The outrage economy might persist indefinitely in its current inflated state, with participants accepting degraded value because they've sunk costs into learning how to operate within it and fear that whatever would replace it might disadvantage them further. Or hybrid outcomes might emerge, where some communities abandon outrage currency while others double down on it, creating increasingly separate moral economies that no longer recognize each other's terms. What remains certain is that current conditions aren't sustainable. You can't run an economy where the primary currency multiplies exponentially while purchasing power declines indefinitely. The mathematics forces correction. The only question is what form that correction takes and who bears its costs.

The deeper question is whether we'll recognize these dynamics. At the same time, we still have agency to influence outcomes, or whether we'll pretend that outrage currency has real value until the system collapses around us. That recognition requires admitting uncomfortable truths: much of what presents as moral witness is actually status competition, genuine commitment to justice often looks nothing like performed outrage, and the infrastructure we've built around moral expression actively undermines the work required to address the injustices we claim to care about. Admitting these truths costs something; it means acknowledging that your own outrage performances might have been currency speculation rather than an authentic moral response. But that acknowledgment is the only path toward rebuilding systems where moral expression actually means something again, where outrage signals real commitment rather than strategic positioning, where the currency of conscience purchases justice rather than just purchasing status.

# Chapter 9: Reclaiming Fairness: Beyond the Performative Facade

Fairness didn't die. It went into witness protection, hiding from the people claiming to defend it.

The machinery of performance consumed everything genuine about justice advocacy and left behind a hollowed-out replica optimized for social media engagement rather than structural change. But fairness, actual fairness, the kind that measures outcomes rather than intentions, that demands consistency rather than selective application, that costs something to pursue, still exists. It operates in spaces the performance economy hasn't colonized yet. The question isn't whether fairness is retrievable. The question is whether we're willing to abandon the theatre that's replaced it and rebuild from principles that actually work.

Reclaiming fairness requires something the current discourse actively discourages: distinguishing between what advances justice and what merely advertises commitment to justice. That distinction has been deliberately obscured because the performance economy profits from conflating the two. When posting the right statement counts as activism, when adopting the correct vocabulary substitutes for policy engagement, when displaying the proper emotional response replaces material support, the system protects itself by making real action and symbolic gesture indistinguishable. The first step toward fairness is recovering the ability to tell them apart. The second step is choosing real action, even when it generates less social approval than a symbolic gesture. The third step is building systems that reward effectiveness rather than performance. None of these steps is complex. All of them are uncomfortable.

## The Return to Outcome Measurement

Start with a principle the performance economy abandoned: judge initiatives by their results, not their rhetoric.

The shift from outcome measurement to intention measurement represents one of the most consequential changes in how social justice operates. Historically, movements evaluated success through material metrics. The Civil Rights Act of 1964 succeeded because it changed who could access public accommodations, employment, and voting, and measurable changes in how resources and power were distributed. The Americans with Disabilities Act succeeded because it mandated physical access modifications that you could photograph, count, and verify. These movements didn't primarily concern themselves with whether people held the right beliefs or used the right language. They concerned themselves with whether disabled people could enter buildings, whether Black applicants got hired, and whether women received equal pay. The measurement was external and verifiable.

Contemporary social justice largely abandoned outcome measurement in favor of process measurement. Did your organization conduct antiracism training? Did your hiring committee use inclusive language in the job posting? Did your leadership issue a statement about recent events? These process measures tell you nothing about whether outcomes changed. You can conduct antiracism training while your organization's racial pay gap widens. You can use inclusive language while your hiring remains demographically unchanged. You can issue statements while your policies perpetuate exactly the inequities you claim to oppose. But process measures are easier; they require less accountability, generate less conflict, and produce more opportunities for consultants to sell services. The performance economy is optimized for process because process is packageable and sellable in ways that genuine outcome transformation isn't.

Reclaiming fairness means returning to outcome discipline. Did your intervention reduce disparity or increase it? Did your policy change who has access to opportunity, or just change who feels good about the status quo? Did your initiative redistribute resources or just redistribute rhetoric? These questions cut through performance instantly. They reveal which efforts actually advance fairness and which efforts advance careers built on talking about fairness. The resistance to outcome measurement is instructive. When you propose evaluating initiatives by their results, advocates of those initiatives often respond with process defenses: "But we implemented best practices." "But we followed the recommended framework." "But we hired the right consultants." These responses reveal the game. If your initiative actually worked, you'd welcome outcome measurement because it would validate your approach. If your initiative only worked at generating the appearance of progress, outcome measurement threatens everything.

The return to outcome measurement requires institutional courage that's currently rare. University administrations that spent millions on diversity infrastructure would need to publish demographic data showing whether those expenditures changed faculty and student composition, retention rates, and graduation rates. Corporations that launched inclusion programs would need to track whether those programs affected promotion rates, pay equity, and leadership diversity over time. Nonprofit organizations that advocate for justice would need to demonstrate whether their advocacy altered the conditions they claim to address. Most won't do this voluntarily because outcome measurement creates accountability, and accountability reveals how much of the current justice industry produces no measurable justice. But fairness demands it anyway.

## Reconstructing Universal Standards

The performance economy replaced universal principles with particularist exceptions, and that replacement needs reversing.

Fairness operates through consistent application of standards across contexts. The same rules apply regardless of who's involved. The same criteria determine outcomes irrespective of the identities of participants. This isn't colorblindness or ignorance of context; it's recognition that justice requires predictability, and predictability involves consistency. When standards shift based on identity, when rules apply selectively based on whose ox is being gored, when identical behaviors receive different judgments depending on the demographics of who's being judged, that's not sophisticated attention to power dynamics. That's corruption of the fairness mechanism itself.

Watch what happens in domains where standards dissolved into identity-dependent applications. Academic peer review once operated on ostensibly universal criteria: methodological rigor, theoretical contribution, empirical support, and logical coherence. Papers stood or fell on those grounds regardless of author identity or political implications. Then came the particularist correction: we must consider whose knowledge we're privileging, whose voices we're amplifying, whose perspectives we're centering.

The correction wasn't wrong to notice that supposedly universal standards had blind spots; they did. But the solution wasn't to maintain rigorous standards while expanding who participates in setting and applying them. The solution became suspending standards entirely when using them would produce politically uncomfortable results. Research with methodological problems gets published if it reaches approved conclusions. Work with logical gaps gets celebrated if it advances the right agenda. Papers that would be rejected for any other author get through review if the author has the right identity credentials. This doesn't fix the original bias; it just replaces one form of corruption with another.

The same pattern repeats in employment decisions, admissions processes, editorial choices, grant allocations, and award selections. Standards get applied rigorously when doing so produces desired outcomes, and get suspended when they don't. This creates precisely what fairness opposes: unpredictability, favoritism, and the sense that identical performance receives different judgment depending on factors unrelated to merit. Defenders argue this corrects for historical injustice, but it doesn't; it perpetuates the mechanism that created injustice in the first place, just with different beneficiaries. If subjective, identity-dependent application of standards was wrong when it disadvantaged marginalized groups, it remains wrong when it advantages them. The principle is what matters, not the direction of the bias.

Reconstructing universal standards doesn't mean ignoring context or pretending power differentials don't exist. It means establishing clear criteria, applying them consistently, and accepting the outcomes even when they're politically inconvenient. It means acknowledging that sometimes the fair answer is "I don't know" rather than forcing a conclusion that fits the narrative. It means recognizing that complexity exists, that reasonable people might disagree, and that adjudicating disagreements requires standards that don't change based on who's winning. This reconstruction faces ferocious resistance because universal standards constrain the powerful, including the newly powerful who benefit from particularist exceptions. But fairness requires it anyway.

## The Rehabilitation of Dissent

Fairness depends on the ability to question claims, challenge conclusions, and propose alternatives without suffering social annihilation.

The current discourse operates on an unstated premise: certain topics have been settled, certain conclusions are beyond dispute, and raising questions about them indicates moral deficiency rather than intellectual curiosity. This premise kills fairness. When challenging a claim, risks being interpreted as attacking the person making it, when requesting evidence for assertions gets treated as denying the lived experience behind them, when proposing alternative explanations triggers accusations of defending injustice, the result isn't justice. It's dogma. And dogma produces injustice with perfect reliability because it eliminates the error-correction mechanisms that fairness requires.

Consider what happens to institutional decision-making when dissent becomes unsafe. A university committee discusses a proposed policy. The policy claims to advance equity but contains provisions that violate procedural fairness. Committee members recognize the problems but remain silent because raising concerns will be interpreted as opposing equity rather than defending due process. The policy passes. It gets implemented. It produces predictable disasters, accusations without evidence, punishment without appeal, and disparate application based on identity. The disasters harm exactly the people the policy claimed to protect. But nobody can say "we told you this would happen" because nobody was permitted to tell you it would happen. The absence of dissent didn't reflect consensus; it reflected fear.

This dynamic repeats across institutions. Journalists know certain stories can't be pursued regardless of evidence because pursuing them violates political orthodoxy.

Researchers know certain findings can't be published irrespective of methodological soundness because they conflict with approved narratives. Administrators know certain decisions can't be questioned regardless of procedural irregularities because the decisions serve the right causes. The silence doesn't indicate agreement. It indicates capture. When the cost of dissent exceeds what most people can bear, professional reputation, social relationships, career advancement, and community belonging disappear. What remains looks like a consensus but functions like coercion.

Rehabilitating dissent requires separating disagreement from harm. Someone questioning whether a particular policy will achieve its stated goals isn't attacking the people the policy claims to help; they're asking whether the policy will actually help them. Someone requesting evidence for empirical claims isn't denying injustice exists; they're trying to ensure responses to injustice are based on an accurate understanding rather than assumption. Someone proposing alternative explanations for patterns isn't defending the status quo; they're trying to identify the actual mechanisms producing unjust outcomes so interventions can target causes rather than symptoms. These distinctions are obvious. The performance economy deliberately collapses them because maintaining the collapse protects initiatives that don't work from criticism that might force improvement.

The way forward requires rebuilding norms that treat disagreement as generative rather than destructive. That means distinguishing between substantive criticism and personal attack. It means demanding arguments address the strongest version of opposing positions rather than the weakest caricatures. It means recognizing that confidence in your conclusions should correlate with how thoroughly you've engaged with counterarguments rather than how successfully you've avoided them. It means accepting that being questioned doesn't constitute harm, being disagreed with doesn't indicate prejudice, and being wrong doesn't destroy your credibility if you correct yourself. None of this is sophisticated. It's basic intellectual honesty, and basic intellectual honesty is what fairness requires.

## The Economics of Attention Redistribution

The performance economy captured discourse by capturing attention. Reclaiming fairness requires redirecting attention from spectacle to substance.

Platform algorithms optimize for engagement, and engagement correlates with emotional intensity rather than practical utility. This creates predictable distortions. Stories about individual villains generate more engagement than analyses of systemic patterns. Outrage about symbolic offenses generates more engagement than documentation of material harms. Calls for punishment create more engagement than reform proposals. The algorithm doesn't care about fairness; it cares about time-on-platform. But the discourse it shapes determines what problems get attention, what solutions get discussed, and what initiatives get resources. When attention systematically flows away from the work that advances fairness toward the spectacle that simulates it, fairness loses by default.

Consider resource allocation across advocacy domains. Initiatives that lend themselves to viral moments attract funding, staff, and organizational energy. Initiatives that require sustained attention to technical policy details struggle for support. This isn't because viral initiatives are less important; sometimes, they address genuinely significant issues. But the allocation doesn't reflect importance or effectiveness. It reflects what captures attention in an attention economy. The result is predictable: advocacy organizations optimize their work for attention generation rather than problem-solving. They develop sophisticated capabilities in narrative construction, symbolic politics, and emotional mobilization. They lose or never develop capabilities in policy analysis, empirical evaluation, and coalition-building across differences. The performance improves. The outcomes don't.

Redirecting attention requires conscious resistance to platform incentives. It means seeking out the detailed policy analysis that will never go viral instead of the hot take designed to. It means reading the hundred-page report on disparate outcomes instead of the thread explaining why someone said something bad. It means following organizations doing unglamorous work on sentencing reform, housing policy, and school funding instead of celebrities announcing their solidarity with causes. It means recognizing that the most important work rarely generates the most compelling content, and adjusting your attention allocation accordingly. This is harder than it sounds because the algorithm fights you at every step, it hides the substantive work, and promotes the spectacular performance. But fairness requires finding the substance anyway.

The shift also requires changing how we evaluate organizations and initiatives. Stop measuring impact through follower counts, viral moments, or media appearances. Start measuring through policy changes, resource distribution, and outcome shifts. Judge advocacy organizations by whether they move legislation, not by whether they move sentiment. Judge initiatives by whether they reduce disparities, not by whether they raise awareness. Judge leaders by whether they build coalitions capable of wielding power, not by whether they build audiences capable of generating engagement. The performance economy trained us to mistake visibility for impact. Still, visibility isn't impact; it's often impact's opposite, capturing resources that could go toward actual change and redirecting them toward spectacle instead.

## The Reconstruction of Trust

Fairness requires trust in institutions, and trust requires that institutions operate predictably according to stated principles rather than political convenience.

The performance economy destroyed institutional trust through a specific mechanism: it made institutions instruments of ideological enforcement rather than neutral arbiters of fair process. When universities abandon due process protections in sexual misconduct cases because maintaining them appears to oppose survivors, they betray their function. When corporations fire employees for political statements unrelated to job performance because keeping them seems to tolerate bigotry, they betray their function. When media organizations suppress stories that undermine preferred narratives because publishing them appears to legitimize harm, they betray their function. Each betrayal happens for understandable reasons, the political pressure is real, the reputational risks are genuine, and the desire to demonstrate alignment with justice is sincere. But each betrayal teaches the same lesson: institutions don't follow their stated principles; they follow political winds. And once that lesson is learned, trust evaporates.

The trust deficit has cascading consequences. When people stop believing institutions will apply rules fairly, they stop cooperating with institutional processes. They lawyer up immediately, they refuse to participate in investigations, and they treat every proceeding as political combat rather than fact-finding. This makes institutions less effective, which drives more process breakdowns, which accelerates the trust collapse. The downward spiral feeds itself. Eventually, you reach a state where institutions maintain formal procedures. Still, nobody believes those procedures will produce fair outcomes, so everyone games the system, which guarantees the system won't produce fair outcomes, which validates everyone's cynicism. Exit is impossible; most people can't opt out of institutional authority. Voice is pointless; complaints get dismissed as defending privilege. The only option is loyalty to whichever faction captures institutional power, and loyalty delivered under those conditions isn't trust, it's submission.

Rebuilding trust requires institutions to recommit to procedural fairness even when it's politically costly. That means maintaining due process protections even when the accused holds unpopular views. It means following the stated criteria even when they produce outcomes that seem unjust through a political lens. It means publishing research that contradicts preferred narratives if the research is methodologically sound. It means making decisions based on established rules rather than current political pressure. This requires courage from institutional leaders, and institutional leaders currently face overwhelming incentives toward cowardice. The administrator who maintains a fair process when doing so appears to tolerate bigotry will be targeted, protested, and possibly removed. The journalist who publishes the uncomfortable story will be accused of causing harm. The researcher who releases inconvenient findings will be characterized as advancing oppression. The professional consequences of procedural integrity are severe.

But the consequences of abandoning it are worse. Institutions that operate as ideological enforcers rather than neutral arbiters lose legitimacy with everyone except true believers, and true believers are always a minority. The majority of people who care about fairness but don't subscribe to every element of current progressive orthodoxy withdraw cooperation. They stop volunteering information, stop participating in processes, and stop believing institutions serve justice rather than faction. The withdrawal doesn't happen loudly through protest. It occurs quietly through disengagement, and disengaged populations are impossible to govern fairly because they don't trust governance itself. Rebuilding that trust requires years of consistent behavior demonstrating that institutions actually follow the principles they claim to operate by. There's no shortcut. Every betrayal of principle for political convenience extends the timeline.

## The Practice of Intellectual Humility

Fairness requires admitting what you don't know and updating beliefs when evidence contradicts them.

The performance economy rewards certainty and punishes ambiguity, which creates systematic bias toward overconfidence. When expressing doubt indicates insufficient commitment to justice, when asking questions gets interpreted as challenging victims, when updating your position based on new information gets characterized as unprincipled flip-flopping, the incentive structure pushes everyone toward maximum confidence regardless of actual epistemic warrant. This produces discourse where people make sweeping claims about complex social phenomena based on minimal evidence, where admitting uncertainty appears as moral weakness, and where changing your mind suggests you're compromised rather than learning. The resulting environment is hostile to truth-seeking because truth-seeking requires exactly what this environment punishes: epistemic humility, willingness to say "I don't know," openness to correction.

Consider what intellectual humility would actually look like in contemporary social justice discourse. It would mean acknowledging that most social science research is methodologically limited in ways that constrain confident causal claims. It would mean recognizing that competing explanations for outcome disparities might all have partial validity, rather than one being obviously right and the alternatives being obviously motivated by bias. It would mean accepting that interventions might not work as intended, that good intentions don't guarantee good outcomes, and that policies designed to help might inadvertently harm. It would mean treating empirical questions as empirical questions rather than moral tests. None of this requires abandoning commitment to justice. It just requires distinguishing between what we know and what we believe, being honest about the strength of evidence supporting various claims, and building arguments that acknowledge complexity rather than pretending it doesn't exist.

The practical implementation faces resistance because intellectual humility looks like political weakness in an environment that treats certainty as virtue. But the alternative, maintaining maximalist claims that evidence doesn't support, ultimately undermines justice advocacy more than humility would. When you make overconfident claims that subsequent evidence refutes, you don't just lose credibility on that specific issue. You lose credibility on everything else you've said. The person who claimed with absolute certainty that X policy would produce Y outcome, only to have X policy produce completely different results, has taught everyone listening not to trust their future certainty; the damage compounds. If you want people to believe you when evidence strongly supports your position, you can't demand they accept you with equal confidence when evidence barely supports it. Intellectual humility isn't retreat from justice; it's the foundation for building durable coalitions based on shared commitment to accuracy rather than shared commitment to narrative.

Practicing intellectual humility also means engaging seriously with uncomfortable data and inconvenient research. When studies produce findings that contradict your preferred explanations, the intellectually honest response isn't to immediately search for methodological problems that would justify dismissing them. It's to examine the research carefully, consider whether it might be correct, and update your confidence accordingly. When someone raises an objection you haven't considered, the intellectually honest response isn't to question their motives. It's to address the substance of the objection. When someone proposes an alternative explanation for patterns you've been attributing to discrimination, the intellectually honest response isn't to accuse them of denying discrimination exists. It's to evaluate whether their alternative explanation better fits the available evidence. This basic standard of intellectual engagement has disappeared from social justice discourse, replaced by motivated reasoning that serves political goals rather than truth-seeking. Reclaiming fairness requires reclaiming truth-seeking even when truth is politically inconvenient.

Fairness isn't lost. It's buried under layers of performance, captured by an economy that profits from its simulation, obscured by discourse optimized for engagement rather than accuracy. But fairness, actual fairness, measured by outcomes and applied consistently, remains intellectually coherent and practically achievable. Reclaiming it requires abandoning the theatre, rebuilding institutions that operate on principle rather than pressure, redistributing attention from spectacle to substance, and recommitting to truth-seeking even when truth complicates the narrative. None of this is easy. All of it is necessary. The alternative is what we have now: a justice discourse that produces injustice, an equity industry that perpetuates inequity, and a moral vocabulary that's lost its connection to the moral reality it supposedly describes. Fairness demands better. We're capable of better. What's missing isn't knowledge or resources, it's the willingness to choose substance over performance when performance offers better social rewards.

# About The Author

Jordan Ellis is a cultural critic and social commentator with a deep interest in identity politics, social justice movements, and the intersection of morality and language in contemporary discourse. With an academic background in sociology and philosophy, Jordan has spent over a decade analyzing how language shapes our understanding of social movements and societal issues. Their work encompasses journalism, public speaking, and academic writing, earning them recognition as a thought leader in discussions surrounding wokeness and performative activism. Jordan has contributed to various publications, sharing insights that challenge conventional perspectives on social justice, urging a focus on practical change over symbolic gestures. Outside of writing, Jordan is an advocate for community engagement and empowerment through grassroots activism, believing that genuine progress stems from collective action rather than individual performance.

# About The Publisher

Welcome to The Book On Publishing

At The Book On Publishing, we believe in rewriting the rules of learning. Whether you're chasing your next big idea, building a better life, or simply curious about what should have been taught in school, you've come to the right place.

We're a platform built for dreamers, doers, and lifelong learners, offering bold, practical books and tools that empower you to take charge of your journey. From real-world skills to mindset mastery, we publish the book on what matters.

No fluff. No lectures. Just what you need to know, delivered with clarity, purpose, and a spark of curiosity.

Start exploring. Start growing. Start writing your story.

Read more at https://thebookon.ca.

# Acknowledgment of AI Assistance

Portions of this book were developed with the support of AI. While every word has been carefully reviewed and refined by the author, AI served as a valuable tool for brainstorming, editing, and structuring ideas. Its assistance helped accelerate the creative process and clarify complex topics.

www.ingramcontent.com/pod-product-compliance
Lightning Source LLC
Chambersburg PA
CBHW060235030426
42335CB00014B/1470